A RAID OVER BERLIN

A miraculous true-life
Second World War survival story

Withdrawn Stock
Dorset Libraries

London-born John Martin volunteered for the RAF as a trainee wireless operator in 1941, aged nineteen.

On completing his training, he was posted to RAF Kermington, in Lincolnshire. Here he crewed Lancaster bombers until, on the night of January 30th, 1944, on only his third operational mission, his plane was brought down over Germany. After a miraculous escape, his parachute opening in the chaos of a disintegrating aeroplane, he was captured and interrogated before being held as a prisoner of war.

After the Allies finally crushed the Nazi regime in the spring of 1945, bringing the war in Europe to an end, John Martin was liberated by British troops and repatriated back to life in Britain. He returned home to his family and was met by his fiancée, Adelaide, who he married shortly after. The couple went on to raise a family. John Martin, now aged ninety-six, lives in Cardigan, Wales.

A RAID OVER BERLIN

A miraculous true-life
Second World War survival story

John Martin

Parthian, Cardigan SA43 1ED
www.parthianbooks.com
First published in 2018
© John Martin 2018
ISBN 978-1-912681-19-8
Editor: Geraint Thomas
Cover image © Imperial War Museum
Cover design: www.theundercard.co.uk
Photos of medals and present day portraits © mgh-photography.co.uk
Typeset by Elaine Sharples
Printed by Gomer Press, Llandysul, Ceredigion
Published with the financial support of the Welsh Books Council.
British Library Cataloguing in Publication Data
A cataloguing record for this book is available from the British Library.

ACKNOWLEDGEMENTS

I would like to give my thanks to my wife, Adelaide, for all her support and encouragement in writing this book. Thanks to Ann and Nick for all the help they have given in many ways. Thanks to Lynda and Jeremy for their encouragement, and to Lynda's Book Circle who sent encouraging comments. Thanks also to our good neighbour, Pauline, for her support and encouragement, and to all the friends who gave support.

To all who suffered in World War Two.

CONTENTS

Prologue

A miraculous escape

Even now, after almost seventy-five years, I still have no idea how I came to be falling through the savaged sky, amidst the smoke, bombs and deadly flak that raged over Berlin, on that fateful night in 1944, but, whether it was an act of God or an unbelievable twist of fate, I have remained ever grateful.

At that moment I had little time to ponder such a question, as Nazi Germany rushed ever closer beneath my feet, nor could I think about our stricken Lancaster MK1 and the rest of my crew – although they too have remained in my thoughts across the decades – as I knew I was far from being in the clear.

I quickly tried to recall the time spent in the classroom in basic training and all the advice we needed to heed when lost behind enemy lines, however, in hindsight, there was little they could have said to prepare me for what was to come.

Of the 125,000 courageous men of Bomber Command, who set off on missions over enemy territory during the Second World War, almost half never returned to their families; thankfully I did but it was to be over a year before I saw my loved ones again.

The memory of that exacting journey, the terror and hardship, panic and uncertainty, has always cast an unwanted shadow in my periphery, like that of a rain cloud menacing a summer's day, but I wish to recall it here, so it is not lost when my passing, so fortunately outfoxed on several occasions, so many years ago, finally catches up with me.

Chapter 1

Joining the Fight

You could blame the naivety of youth for my enlisting in the Royal Air Force, but I was to grow up considerably in the troubled Second World War years that followed.

Being a London boy, from a working-class background, I saw the RAF as an opportunity to better myself, to get into a profession that had been previously denied young men such as myself and, in September 1941, not long after turning nineteen, I quit my job as an apprentice coachbuilder and, alongside my friend Eddy Stevens, signed up to train as a RAF wireless operator.

I wasn't seeking to become a hero or itching to risk my life for King and Country; in fact, like so many of my contemporaries, I did not perceive the war as dangerous and likely to claim our lives. We reasoned the horrors of the First World War were ancient history and, therefore, not connected with the present war. Also, the excitement of flying an aircraft far outweighed any thoughts of danger.

So, fuelled by the thoughts of flying and the ambition to better myself, I attended evening classes with the Air

Training Corps in Wembley. Having left Wesley Road Senior Boys School at the age of fourteen, I found the maths hard going and therefore was pleased to receive the extra tuition provided by my friend Eddy, who had enjoyed the good fortune to be able to remain at school until he was sixteen and gain a higher standard of education.

Eventually, with our classes successfully completed, I attended the Aircrew Selection at RAF Cardington in Bedfordshire. Here, although keen to be a wireless operator, I was selected by the Aircrew Selection Board to train as a pilot. I really felt as though I had fallen on my feet and was billeted in a sumptuous flat in St John's Wood and attended lectures in the famous Board Room at Lord's Cricket Ground. My new career saw me experiencing the luxurious side of the RAF. This was something that, even in my wildest dreams, I had never imagined being a part of.

My bubble was soon to be burst, however, when I was told that, although I had been selected to train as a pilot, due to a shortage of bomb aimers, the entire intake would embark on training to address this crewing shortage. I did not accept this operational decision willingly and, after some persuasion, it was decided I could train as a wireless operator, as was my original wish. Little did I know that those turn of events may well have saved my life as both the pilot and bomb aimer in my future crew were to pay the ultimate price for their part in the war.

The next stage of my training was at Signals Schools, which involved moving around the country to specialist establishments. The first part, learning to be a ground-based wireless operator, was undertaken at Blackpool and then Yatesbury in Wiltshire. The next move was to Madley in Herefordshire, to learn the air operating procedures. The final move was to Stormy Down in south Wales, for air gunnery, from where I emerged wearing an Air Gunner's beret and sergeant's stripes, or tapes as they were known.

I was to get my first taste of an unwanted side of life in the RAF while in Signals School: the attentions of the Flight Sergeant. Anyone who has been in the RAF will tell you that, during basic training, everyone lives in fear of the Flight Sergeant. He was not a technical man by any means; he was there for disciplinary purposes, and one of his objectives was to make you realise that you were no longer a human being, and that when he said 'Move' you moved.

Flight Sergeant aside, I enjoyed my training and, in the spring of 1943, I was posted to the Advanced Air Training School at RAF Llandwrog in north Wales where the reception from the local inhabitants was somewhat cool. Rumours were circulating amongst the crews of the problems encountered during the construction of the station a few months earlier. Some of the indigenous population, many of them isolated from the rest of Britain in this remote corner of north

Wales, did not want an aircraft training school and 'foreigners' in their community. So, they embarked on attempts to sabotage the building of the station – allegedly, led by their vicar.

It was at this time, at RAF Llandwrog, when I heard some very bad news. My friend, Eddy Stevens, had been killed in a flying accident during the final months of his training. I wasn't to know, at that time, that the war had only just began to claim the lives of my friends.

From Llandwrog I was posted to RAF Cottesmore in Leicestershire, with its complement of Wellington MKICs. I would finally get to fly an operational aircraft. My first experience of a Wellington, however, would be in one that was firmly fixed to the ground. Before any flying was attempted the aircrews had to familiarise themselves with the aircraft's layout and we were given instructions in a wing-less fuselage section of a Wellington, known as a dummy fuselage.

More importantly, it was at Cottesmore that I was to meet a small group of people who would hold my life in their hands – my aircrew. The process of forming the aircrews of Bomber Command followed what was perhaps an unusual and undisciplined path for a military body like the RAF and ran against the usual practice of giving and receiving orders. Interestingly, the crews were instructed to form by mutual agreement amongst each other – rather than direction by a senior officer. One individual, typically the pilot, but not necessarily so, would choose his own aircrew. In the close confines of a wartime aircraft, where the aircrew need to work as a close-knit team and where the lives of each are dependent on the actions of the others, a closely bonded team was essential. Fortunately, the RAF realised that the best way to accomplish this was to let the crews form themselves.

A Lancaster's aircrew was made up of seven members, each with a unique role to play but each dependent upon his fellow crew members. The whole process of taking-off, reaching the target, dropping its payload and returning safely home rested upon the aircrew's ability to work as a team.

Firstly, you had the pilot who flew the aircraft and called all the shots throughout the operation: in the team analogy he was the skipper. Our pilot, Jimmy Tosh, was Scottish, and came from Dundee originally but had joined the RAF from the Metropolitan Police in London. He was a good pilot, nice and steady.

Our navigator was another Scotsman, Hugh Mosen, but we all called him Jock. He was a charted accountant and had been working in Poland before the war but, of course, had to return home. He was actually sent out to South Africa to do his training.

A marvellous thing, that perhaps the general public didn't know, was that RAF aircrew training was taking place all over the world. In Bomber Command we had the privilege of training with, or even being in a crew with, men from all parts of the then great British Empire. The larger countries had their own air forces, namely the Royal Australian Air Force, the Royal Canadian Air Force, the Royal New Zealand Air Force, the Royal Indian Air Force and the Royal South African Air Force, while the smaller countries in the Empire, such as Jamaica, were grouped with the RAF but wore a shoulder flash indicating their nationality. It was an extreme example of co-operation, organisation and determination. Because all the training was co-ordinated, wherever in the world it was done, we could all come together and work as a crew.

As one would imagine, being the navigator, Jock was tasked with keeping the aircraft on course, reaching the target and then getting us home.

Both Jimmy and Jock were older than the rest of us; they were closer to thirty while the rest of us were in our early twenties.

David Alletson, our flight engineer, came from Nottingham, and was an engineer by civilian trade, having worked in coal-mining before the war. He was a good lad; they were all good lads. His main job was to oversee the aircraft's mechanical, hydraulic, electrical and fuel systems, and also assist the pilot with take-off and landing.

Reg Morris, our bomb aimer, was another Londoner, like myself, who did part of his training in Canada. He was very easy to get along with – we all had to be; you couldn't have anyone thinking that they were better or worse than the rest, or miserable.

Reg had a particularly crucial role as he took control of the aircraft when it was on its bombing run, lying flat in the nose of the aircraft, giving directions until the bombs were released. He also acted as the reserve pilot.

Then came our gunners. Bob Brown, our mid-upper gunner, was Canadian, from the Royal Canadian Air Force, and was trained in Canada, although he did the last bit of his training in Britain. And Dick Walton, our rear turret gunner, was from Wallasey, just across the Mersey from Liverpool.

Both were physically separated from the other crew members and confined to their respective turrets for the whole flight. Their main duty was to advise the pilot of enemy aircraft movements – to allow him to take evasive action – and to defend the aircraft against enemy fighters.

As the wireless operator, I was tasked with transmitting and receiving all messages between the aircraft and our base, as well as assisting the navigator by taking loop bearings, turning the IFF (Identification: Friend or Foe) set on or off at given points, and ensuring the "flying rations" were on board, which were vital for long flights.

*

I had been at Cottesmore about four weeks when the news came that everyone would be transferred to a brand-new station – RAF Husbands Bosworth in Leicestershire. No official reason was given for this posting but rumour amongst the aircrews at the time said that it was because the Americans were going to be based at Cottesmore and history confirmed this to be true.

Flying at Bosworth began in August 1943 even though the construction work was still not entirely complete. There was now immense pressure from Bomber Command to build and operate Operational Training Units as quickly as possible to enable air strikes on Germany's industrial cities to be carried out.

Many take-offs and landings, known as circuits and bumps, were undertaken, in Wellington bombers, to hone the skills of the pilot and crew. I have never forgotten the intensity of the training and the endless circuits and bumps which were undertaken day after day in order to perfect the crew's take-off and landing skills; but it was not without its humorous moments.

After each landing the pilot contacted the control tower to broadcast the standard radio message, 'Clear of main runway.'

Now Jimmy, our pilot, was the archetypal Mr Cool and was every bit as calm and collected as the pilots portrayed in wartime films. One day when we were doing circuits and bumps, the aircraft had just touched down when, suddenly, it lurched uncontrollably to the port. A sixty-second white-knuckle ride followed as our Wellington left the runway then, eventually, after crossing the airfield, came to a halt on the perimeter track.

Without a pause, reflection or expletive, and completely unfazed, Jimmy called up the control and said, 'Clear of runway.'

'So I see,' came back the reply from the controller.

Another part of training was being positioned on the airfield, in a mobile caravan, to observe take-offs and landings. One day, as I was in the caravan, an unannounced light aircraft landed and taxied to a halt in front of me. The young pilot, who I recognised as being American, leaned out of his cockpit and called out in a casual manner, 'Hey Bud. Can you give me the bearing for Oxford?'

I was about to call control when the phone rang. The in-coming call was from a very edgy and tense controller, asking exactly who this intruder was? I felt relieved I had not spoken first. The controller barked at me, 'Tell him to report to me, now.'

I had learnt a vital wartime lesson – always be suspicious of strangers.

*

It was shortly after arriving at RAF Husbands Bosworth, with my new aircrew, that I was to form another, far more important and longer lasting relationship – with my future wife.

Adelaide was in the Women's Auxiliary Air Force (WAAF) and, at the time, stationed at RAF Little Rissington in Gloucestershire, which was many miles away from Bosworth. Fortunately for me, she was from a small village near my base called Sibbertoft, and was home on leave. As it was a Saturday night, she had cycled to nearby Welford to attend a dance in the village hall with her friend. I had also decided to attend the dance – such an alignment of chance must have meant we were destined to meet.

I can still remember the first time I set eyes on her; she was wearing an attractive civilian dress and I plucked up the courage to ask her out. To my relief she said yes and I'm proud to say we are still together this very day – but it was by no means an easy courtship.

Following the dance, I asked if I could walk her home. She agreed but when she told me that she lived in Sibbertoft, at least three miles away, I realised I had been presented with a problem; I did not have a car, a motorcycle or even a bicycle. Eventually, a solution was agreed: I would pedal Adelaide's bike standing up and she would sit, legs outstretched, on the saddle. And so, in this rickshaw-manner, I took my date home.

With Adelaide and her bicycle safely returned, and our next meeting arranged, it seemed a simple enough matter to walk back to the base. But the night was dark and I soon found myself disorientated. I was in a strange environment, being more familiar with navigating the streets of London than the open countryside, and it was many hours before I finally returned to my bunk.

I eagerly counted down the days to our next meeting but I had no idea at that stage that there was competition. There was a young pilot who, like me, had just arrived at Husbands Bosworth for the Operational Training Course. I had already got to know him, and liked him. He had just come from completing his Advanced Flying Unit course at Little Rissington where Adelaide was stationed and they had already met.

At this same time Adelaide was home on leave at nearby Sibbertoft and they met up again. A "date" was made when he would call at her house in the village. In the meanwhile she met me at the dance and, forgetting her previous engagements, invited me to visit her – same day, same place.

When her mother heard about this she was very concerned, but it all worked out well. I got there first and had a very pleasant walk in the woods with Adelaide while the young pilot, arriving later, was treated to a good night out at the village pub and was enjoying talking to her father when we arrived back. There were no hard feelings; in fact we kept in touch, remaining friends for many years.

That young pilot was also shot down during the Berlin raids and suffered very badly from frostbite.

Having chosen me, eventually, due to our individual postings future meetings were few and far between and we had to content ourselves with conveying our feelings for one another through exchanges of letters; there were no mobile phones, of course, and any phones available at RAF stations for social use were so much in demand that it was impossible to pre-arrange a call.

We both realised that we may have to wait for the war to run its course before our relationship could develop, as there were no certainties in love, especially if your bloke was preparing to fly in a bomber over Germany – prophetic thoughts indeed.

*

Having completed my training at Bosworth I was posted to a conversion unit where the crew learned to fly four-engine planes: Halifax, Stirling and Lancasters. Here we joined up with the mid-upper gunner and the flight engineer. In January of 1944 we relocated to an operational base called RAF Kirmington, in Lincolnshire, where the war was about to get very real for myself and my aircrew as we were to embark on operation flights in a Lancaster bomber.

Even today, catch sight of one of the two remaining airworthy Lancaster Bombers (as far as I am aware there is only one airworthy Lancaster in the UK, the other is in Canada) heralded by its four Rolls-Royce Merlin piston engines – I was once told by a jet pilot, one of two people who were working with the Lancaster that would become part of the Battle of Britain memorial flight, that he talks to his engines. Each one, he said, has its own individual character – and you will gaze on in awe of this breath-taking instrument of war. To many, it is a true icon of the Second World War, having earned its reputation the hard way as the RAF's principal heavy bomber during the latter half of the conflict – but I have to say there were plenty of other bombers, such as the Wellington, Halifax and Stirling, that did exceptional jobs and, in my opinion, never received the credit they deserved.

Having praised the Lancaster, I must confess that our first one, AS-S2, was nothing to write home about, having gone through the mangle a number of times. It was the oldest most battered thing in our squadron; nobody wanted it but, as we were the new crew, we had to take it. I remember the Flight Sergeant in charge of the maintenance saying, 'There's no need to bring this one back.' But we did. We flew it to Berlin; it got hit a little bit with flak. On our second mission we got hit badly by flak and it wasn't fit to fly after that.

As a result, we weren't supposed to fly on the night of Sunday, January 30, 1944, because we didn't have an aircraft, but then our flight commander said, 'The Old Man says you have to take our aircraft tonight.' Before we went he added, 'Don't bend it; it's a new one.' He didn't see it again. And neither did we.

Chapter 2

Shot down in flames

Until you actually get on an operational squadron, you don't know what you are letting yourself in for. You see that so-and-so didn't come back and you soon realise what your own chances of coming back are – and you are scared.

Figures published many years after the war revealed that of the seven-man aircrew of a Lancaster, the average number to survive after being shot down was less than two.

There was always apprehension, but it was worse for the Wing Commander's crew who had done twenty-seven operations and were due to be rested at thirty. The stress as they waited to reach thirty missions was dreadful; they were like a group of old men. It was terrible. To make matters worse, the Wing Commander wouldn't go on every trip – the top brass wanted him on the squadron for a long time, so he only flew one in three or four missions – and there's his poor crew, waiting desperately to complete the full quota. To this day I don't know whether they finished in one piece or not.

However, it doesn't matter how many missions you fly, you never gain in confidence as you see people who had flown perhaps eighteen or twenty missions, yet the next time they don't come back. There's no comfort in saying, *I've done X amount*; there's no knowing what's going to happen to you.

When you heard that someone you knew hadn't come back you just had to bury your thoughts. There was no use asking what had happened because you knew you wouldn't get an answer. That's it; you just had to take it. The only good thing was, you didn't have long to think about it because the next mission always came – if you were lucky, that is.

*

That night our target was Berlin – it was always Berlin. We were in the middle of what was termed the Battle of Berlin and everybody was sick to death when the target was revealed as Berlin again. The defences over Berlin were very heavy and often you had a long land flight to get there; you would never go the same route twice. Or come back the same way.

The first you know about a mission is in the morning, when someone says, 'Operations are on tonight.' Nobody would know where to, other than the Group Captain and Squadron Commander. The mechanics, though, could tell you whether you were going on a long or short trip, by the amount of fuel they put into the aircraft. Then, at around 14.00 hours, you are called to briefing. That's when you know where you are going.

On that particular occasion, when they put a target map of Berlin up, everyone went, 'Oh hell. We're not going there *again*?' The language was something else. But there you are; you did what you were told.

*

We took off at around 17.00 hours, as it was just about getting dark. It was a long seven-hour trip and for six of them we were over enemy territory. No mission is ever just routine. The other times we went, we hit the flak as soon as we'd crossed the North Sea and got into Holland. We were under flak the whole time, and had to contend with fighters, of course. That night we had a fairly long sea crossing and then went across Denmark and came into Berlin from the north so that we wouldn't be under flak for too long.

I suppose the wireless operator, to use a modern term, could be described as a bit of a loner while on a mission as, for most of the flying time, you are isolated from the intercom system. You would not hear any crew patter; therefore, you would not know of anything going on inside or outside the aircraft, unless you were directly involved.

As far as I was concerned, as the clock reached 20.00 hours, everything had gone well. According to the time, I knew that we would be just to the north-west of the big city and coming up to the target.

I was occupied at this time on the wireless set doing what, if I remember correctly, was codenamed Tinselling. This was to listen out on the receiver, covering frequencies given at briefing, and trying to pick up enemy ground-to-fighter patter. If successful, you would then tune back the transmitter and swamp the frequency with the noise of one of your aircraft's engines. It was just possible to carry out Tinselling while standing under the astrodome (the distinctive Perspex dome to the rear of the cockpit canopy) and reaching backwards to twiddle the knobs. It was a bit of a stretch, but it allowed me to look out for enemy fighters in the extreme danger area to the rear of the aircraft, thus assisting our gunners.

I was doing this until just seconds before we were attacked. I looked back at the clock and was alarmed to see the time was 20.10 hours. I moved in great haste back into my seat and retuned the receiver to receive the Group Broadcast, which was most important.

This action, only prompted by the time, certainly saved my life because within seconds of getting seated, and before having time to adjust the set, cannon shells were ripping past my right arm and exploding, showering green burning phosphorous everywhere. If I had remained standing under the astrodome I would have been right in the path of them.

The Aural Monica, a tail warning radar device, was bleeping out a warning that aircraft were approaching from behind and below. It is highly likely that both our gunners were firing. The noise was deafening.

I knew our aircraft was severely damaged and immediately switched onto the intercom to hear the skipper giving the order, 'Bail out. Bail out.' The navigator, Jock Mosen, and I moved as one man to grab our parachute packs and clip them on.

Following the emergency drill of evacuation, I made to go back down the fuselage in order to jump out of the rear doors after the mid-upper gunner, but upon opening the bulkhead door, at the rear of the cockpit, I was confronted by fierce flames. The whole of the fuselage, between the main spar and just forward of the mid-upper turret, was ablaze. I instantly decided that my only chance was to slam the door shut again. Although by this stage of the war the original steel armour plate had been replaced by plywood, this did provide some psychological comfort and would have acted as some sort of firebreak.

I then turned to follow the bomb aimer, navigator, pilot and engineer out of the emergency escape hatch in the nose.

In the split second that I had the bulkhead door open, I had seen, through the flames, what appeared to be heavy damage to the mid-upper turret. The whole thing was leaning over to starboard. Amazingly, I saw the mid-upper gunner, Bob Brown, climbing out of it.

I could see nothing of what happed to Dick Walton in the rear turret. Sadly, he must have taken the direct stream of fire from a fighter – he would have been firing back until the last.

It soon became obvious that the bail-out from the cockpit was not going according to the drill. In retrospect, I think the bomb aimer, Reg Morris, had been badly wounded or even killed laying in his position down in the nose and over the escape hatch. It would have been very difficult for the other crew members to move him from above, especially as by this time the aircraft was in a steep dive. The pilot, Jimmy Tosh, quite correctly had left his seat to await his turn to jump. I could see him and the engineer, David Alletson, waiting to get down into the nose. The navigator, Jock Mosen, would have been further down and out of sight.

I did not feel any urge to join them – perhaps I could sense the hopelessness of the situation and I remember, rather stupidly it would seem, having the strong feeling that I should not rightly be there and that I must stand back while they had their chance of escape.

The flames I had encountered in the fuselage must have frightened me conclusively because I did not think of trying to escape that way again. Instead I struggled forward, sat in the pilot's seat and pulled on the controls, in an effort to get the aircraft out of the dive. I knew immediately that this was useless as the stick just flopped about; the enemy fire must have disabled the mechanism. I then stood up on the pilot's seat and, with a big effort, tried to slide back the emergency escape hatch, but the cockpit roof was so badly damaged the hatch would not move.

During the time I was doing this – it would only be a few seconds – I could see that still no one had been able to get out from the cockpit. It must have been at this moment that I thought I was going to die because I became remarkably calm. I shuffled back to my table and pressed the two buttons that would have detonated the IFF (Identification Friend or Foe) set to prevent it from falling into enemy hands – I should already have done this before starting to bail out.

I didn't have time to add another fear to my list – that of our own bombs exploding. The standard payload was a bomb called the Cookie, which weighed 4,000 pounds, and six or eight 1,000 pounders, and then a lot of incendiary bombs. We hadn't dropped our load before we were hit; we were just about to go into the target. When the skipper knew that we had been hit pretty badly he would have ordered the bomb aimer to jettison. I have no idea if he did or not because there was too much going on at that point in time. Normally you would know when the bombs are dropped because the aircraft lifts as the weight is lost

– I hadn't felt this but we were in a dive and, as I have said, such thoughts never entered my mind; I had far bigger fears to contend with.

I remember the aircraft diving even more steeply and also that I could no longer move at all. I thought of home, my fiancée and my mother. What would people at home say when they heard what had happened to me? I thought, still quite calmly.

The next thing I remember was seeing a huge red flash – I didn't register any noise of an explosion – then I blacked out.

I became semi-conscious momentarily and saw a huge piece of aircraft sail by very close, while having a sensation of spinning over and over.

It could have been the jolt of the parachute opening that brought me back to something like consciousness. I knew nothing of pulling the ripcord, although of course I must have done so, unless somehow the D-ring had got caught on a piece of wreckage as the aircraft disintegrated.

I was then dangling on the end of my chute – I could not believe I had escaped. I thought how quiet it was; I could hear a dog barking far below and after a few seconds the German all clear siren blowing in the distance. I soon realised that my parachute harness had been ripped off from my left side and that I must be careful not to lean over or I may fall out.

I remember looking down and thinking I was about to fall into a canal – it was, in fact, a main road which was wet and illuminated by the moon. I would have been grateful to drop anywhere.

I shall never forget how lucky I was – we would have been flying at about 20,000 feet before being attacked, but I reached the ground very quickly after the chute opened. At a guess I would say this happened at little more than 1,000 feet.

I tried to remember the parachute landing drill upon hitting the ground. I was very dazed and was being dragged along by my billowing canopy. I was very slow to react. Eventually I came to a halt and after collapsing my chute and unclipping the harness, I stood up. I had no idea of time but found, to my great relief, that I was still in one piece, even if a bit knocked about. Both my knees were very swollen, my legs and head were gashed, and I had suffered a very painful shoulder. I could walk with difficulty and after a few steps realised I had lost one of my boots.

*

Slowly I was able to think about what I should do next. I had landed in a field in a semi-rural area quite close to the road. There was a stack of hay or straw nearby which seemed to be the obvious place to hide my chute and harness – in retrospect this location would have been obvious to the Germans as well.

I urged myself to get away from the area as quickly as

possible, to stand any chance of evading capture, so I turned away from the fires of Berlin. Mistakenly, I went onto the road and was immediately challenged by two soldiers armed with rifles and bayonets. I was in no position to argue.

I was taken to a hut, not far away on the opposite side of the road, and once inside I could see the soldiers were in fact Luftwaffe personnel, more than likely members of a searchlight unit. They were quite kind to me and immediately sent for a medical sergeant who gave me a good deal of time and attention before finally dressing my gashes in paper bandages. I was given coffee and led to understand that I would be collected by higher authority shortly. I thanked them and took the opportunity of giving away some loose change from my pockets that I should not have been carrying in the first place, thinking that it could not then be used for any other purpose than as souvenirs for the several onlookers, who by this time had gathered to see the Englander.

I was taken by car to what I presumed to have been the area Headquarters of the surrounding searchlight units. I was led upstairs and ushered into a large room where I was confronted by a sergeant who, to my surprise, was holding my parachute. This was given back to me and I was told to lie down on it on the floor while the sergeant sat at a desk and listened to German military music whilst keeping a very careful eye on me for the rest of the night.

Early the next morning I was moved into a wooden hut, which was part of the living quarters of the unit's personnel. They showed great interest in me as they went about their off-duty tasks. It would be stand down time now, I thought, as the hut was occupied by some eight or ten men. They were generally kind to me and I was surprised by how many of them could attempt some English conversation. I was told by more than one of them, 'For you the war is over.' They all sounded quite envious, I thought.

In the early afternoon I was told that I was to be collected and taken into Berlin, and, in a short while, I was escorted into the street. It was only at this stage that I became aware that the unit was based inside a pub, which accounted for the smell about which I had been wondering.

Despite a great feeling of trepidation, I was delighted to see at the kerbside the longest Mercedes car I had ever seen, with two very smart looking Luftwaffe officers in the front, and, seated in the back, David Alletson, showing all the arrogance of Field Marshal Goring himself. Despite his bandaged head he grinned broadly upon seeing me being escorted out. (We later discovered that although Bob Brown had also managed to get out, he was wounded quite badly in the legs and so would have been taken to a hospital.)

Seeing our exchange one of the officers immediately took out his pistol and challenged in good English, 'So you two know each other?' We hoped we had convinced him otherwise. The officer in the passenger seat nursed his pistol for the whole of the journey and we were forbidden to speak to each other.

As we were driven to Tempelhof Airfield we were pleased to notice quite a lot of bomb damage along the way and also, on arrival, to find the airfield buildings were also showings signs of damage. I think we spent two nights at Tempelhof, in a cellar, and were later joined by several other RAF aircrew, mostly looking as knocked about as we were.

The whole party was then moved off by train to Frankfurt am Main and taken to Dulag Luft for interrogation. I must recount an incident during the journey that could have been very nasty for all of us. We had been travelling in ordinary passenger trains and had been warned, by those of our escort who could speak English, to conceal our identities as much as possible because the civilian population were extremely hostile towards Allied airmen.

This we managed to do until nearly at the end of the journey. We were awaiting road transport at Frankfurt station to take us to Dulag Luft, when a railway plate-layer leapt up from the track and aimed a blow with his hammer at one of our party. This incident drew the attention of many of the other civilians on the crowded platform and they surged en masse towards us with obvious intentions. Fortunately, the sergeant in charge of the escort, or feldwebel as I was beginning to learn, was quick to sum up the situation, and pushed us all against a wall while arranging his men in the front of us, forming a protective semicircle.

The escort raised their automatic weapons to keep the irate civilians at bay. After what seemed an age, and by making it quite clear, even to our non-German ears, that he would not hesitate to open fire, the feldwebel was able to disperse the crowd. I will always be grateful to that man, although I can now well appreciate the feelings of those civilians. Looking back, presumably he was just anxious to deliver us in one piece to the infamous Dulag Luft, the place we had heard so much about from intelligence during aircrew training.

Chapter 3

Interrogation

Dulag Luft was a specialised transit camp set up by the Luftwaffe, in the suburbs of Frankfurt am Main, to interrogate all captured Allied airmen before they were transferred to the permanent camps dotted around German territory.

We were informed during aircrew training about some of the methods used by the staff there to extract the information they were seeking. During lectures given by RAF Intelligence, we were constantly assured by them that, according to the Geneva Convention, name, number and rank were the only details a prisoner of war was obliged to disclose to the enemy. However, we were also warned how skilled the interrogators at Dulag Luft would be in gaining the information they were seeking, and how they might get a prisoner to talk; typically, pretending friendship and showing what would appear to be a genuine concern that 'your folks at home would not know that you were safe'.

'We could inform them,' they might say, 'but we must have a few more details to make this possible.' Then as the conversation went on, questions like, 'What was your squadron?', 'What type of aircraft were you in?', 'What was your bombload?' and 'What was your target?', would be slipped in when you were off your guard.

'Don't get drawn into a seemingly innocent conversation', was the strong advice always given. We were also warned of the extensive use of microphones at Dulag Luft and, shockingly, the presence of one or two RAF personnel who had turned traitor. Still wearing their uniforms, they mingled with new prisoners, trying to get information for their German masters. Absolutely disgraceful, but true.

Benefiting from being forewarned, I felt prepared for that type of interrogation when it came. However, all due to my own carelessness, I was to be subjected to something quite different. Before going to briefing for the raid, I took the opportunity to have a wash and came away leaving my identity discs hanging on a peg in the washroom. I did not miss them until just before take-off, and did not mention the fact to anyone, as it was too late to do anything about it. Little did I know then what the consequences of this would be, as it was to be used very strongly against me at Dulag Luft.

*

The journey from Frankfurt railway station to the interrogation centre was made, surprisingly, by tramcar but, with us prisoners as the only passengers, our guards had full control. On the way we could see that the bomb damage inflicted by the Allies was dreadful. It was quite extraordinary by comparison to what I had seen during the earlier days of the London Blitz, and more recently, in Berlin. Whole areas, not individual buildings, had been flattened by the United States Air Force's method of carpet bombing.

Our party arrived, thankfully without further civilian interference, and we were quickly escorted into what must have been the main entrance of Dulag Luft. Here we were immediately subjected to the first instance of Applied Psychology.

A pane of glass had been deliberately broken in one of the windows and the hole stuffed-up with a bunch of the aluminium foil strips that were being dropped by our bombers, in certain areas, to foil the enemy radar. It was known to us by the code name Window (it was later referred to as Chaff). The implication here, of course, was, 'We know what you call this stuff and you thought it was a well-guarded secret, didn't you?'. Childish, but it did have some effect on me; as it was meant to do so.

We were immediately singled off and I was led into a room staffed by three or four very arrogant Luftwaffe airmen. I was ordered to strip everything off. With no consideration given to any of my injuries, I was then forced to stand on one side of the room while my clothes were thoroughly searched by two of the airmen. I could sense that their objective was partly to ridicule me as much as possible and make me feel totally humiliated. They made a great show of letting me see they knew exactly where to look for the passport-type photograph, that was sewn into the waistband of my battledress, and another great exhibition was made of cutting off one of the buttons that would also serve as a compass. The passport photograph and the buttons were designed to enable us to forge documents and enable us to escape should the opportunity arise. They then made a great act of gloatingly producing a cigarette, lighting it, then blowing the smoke in my face. 'We Germans have everything, you see,' they might as well have said. They were certainly well trained to do this job, unless this was their natural behaviour.

When they had finished thoroughly searching my clothes, they threw them back at me and then, showing their ignorance, made fun of my fine silk and wool long johns that had recently been issued to counteract the cold during flying duties. 'We modern Germans stopped wearing these old-fashioned things years ago,' was what they implied here. (Actually, they were a great comfort at all times during a cold winter on a north Lincolnshire airfield.)

Then the door was opened by two armed guards and I was marched off along what seemed to be endless corridors, to what was to be my cell for the next nine days. I had barely got inside when the door was slammed shut and locked. It was the start of the most miserable, lonely and anxious time of my life.

The cell was only just big enough to accommodate a narrow bed and to leave just enough room at the side to allow access to it. At the far end of the cell, high up in the wall, was a small barred window. On the bed, in a heap, were two or three dirty looking blankets and a rough pillow. I was to learn during my stay as a prisoner of war that no blankets issued to prisoners of the Germans gave much protection from the cold. There was a book on the bed and although it was in English I never felt that I wanted to read it. I got onto the bed, because there was nowhere else to be, and lay down. There was no sound of any description from the adjoining cells and I knew I was utterly alone.

I remained isolated in my misery for perhaps two hours before hearing the noise of some activity in the corridor. Then someone unlocked the door and passed in a small enamel vessel, containing what I could by now identify by its smell as Ersatzkaffee, an inferior grain coffee, and two thin slices of the very dark, sour tasting bread that I never thought I would ever consider eating, let alone crave, as I was to do during the very hungry days I was to endure as a prisoner of war.

*

Since being blown out of the aircraft I had remained in a state where I think I had never fully regained consciousness. For some days, if someone spoke to me, the voice appeared to come from an unexpected direction. I suppose it was caused by the shock or concussion, or perhaps both. Even so, I remained conscious of the fact that I was unbelievably lucky to have escaped with my life and to be so lightly injured. I kept thinking of the crew. I knew that David the engineer was OK and thought Bob, the mid-upper gunner, would have stood a very good chance of getting out. Sadly, I had seen no sign of Dick, the rear gunner, reaching back into the fuselage to get his parachute, as he would have done had he been able to do so. His turret would almost certainly have been the prime target of the attacking fighters.

Our pilot, navigator and bomb aimer, trapped down in the nose, would have stood little chance of being blown clear, as David and I were. I thought about them continuously as I lay in my cell, but knew better than to enquire about them now, as this would have almost certainly connected me to an aircraft and to a squadron, which might have been information of which my interrogators would make use.

I must have slept for some time before being awakened by the noise in the corridor when two more thin slices of the black bread were passed to me. I was to learn that I had now received two thirds of the daily standard food ration for POWs in Germany. The remaining part was at midday, consisting of a bowl of swede soup which was no more than boiled swede and three small potatoes. This inadequate ration alone would have resulted in slow starvation, unless, before that, because of weakness, prisoners would have succumbed to disease.

We were kept alive by International Red Cross food parcels. I will never cease to be grateful for them. They came from Britain (jointly with The Order of St John) Canada and the USA. Especially appreciated was an occasional bulk consignment of food sent by the British Farmers of the Argentine. They were largely Welsh settlers there, I was to learn many years later.

Shortly after my first full day in the cell I became aware of a large radiator, running for almost the full length of the bed on the opposite wall, because it was throwing out far more heat than was necessary for comfort and there was no way of controlling it. As the day went on the heat became almost unbearable. This continued until late in the afternoon when it stopped, and the cell became cold, very cold. This happened every day and night for the rest of my stay. It must have been another form of psychology applied to make life even more uncomfortable. I learned to get some relief from this in the day by lying on the floor beside the bed, with my head at the door. This allowed me to breathe in the cold air that streamed beneath it.

There was still no sign, as the hours went by on that first day, of anyone occupying the cells on either side of me. The only sound of activity was made by, what I guessed to be, the guards marching along the corridor in their heavy boots. Then, at about midday, the heavy boots halted, in full military fashion, right outside. The door was flung open to reveal two armed guards. One of them ordered, 'Out,' and I was marched off to face my first interrogation.

I was led into a large room and the guards withdrew. I was kept waiting while a smartly dressed Luftwaffe officer sat at a desk, appearing to study some papers. Obviously, as I see it now in my comparatively old aged wisdom, he was applying more psychology. After what seemed an age he motioned me to sit down opposite him. More time was allowed to tick away before he played his master card.

'I don't think you are an airman at all,' he said, 'I think you are an agent, dropped for espionage purposes.' He sat and savoured the effect of this bombshell for several more minutes, before reminding me that I was not wearing RAF identity discs. I tried to defend myself against this charge by pointing out that I was wearing RAF uniform. He dismissed this by saying, 'I can go to Paris and buy any amount of those on the black market,' meaning that my uniform stood for nothing.

He then said, 'You do not appear to belong to an aircrew either.' His accusations were terrifying, but at the same time, I thought, 'He knows about David.'

I was returned to my cell, no doubt to be given time to dwell on my predicament.

Eventually the door was flung open once more and I was led back to my tormentor. As I entered his room he was again studying some papers, and again kept me waiting in terror while he chose the moment to order me to sit.

His acting was as good as his command of the English language, because even before he said a word, I felt doomed.

'I am still convinced you have been dropped for espionage purposes,' he alleged when he was ready. Then he left me again in misery while he slowly gathered up the papers he had been studying, making me think that that was his final decision. I sat there in increasing terror thinking he was about to summon the guards to take me away to face the firing squad.

But next came some relief when he suddenly said, 'Right, if you are who you claim to be, tell me the places where you were trained?'

I refused to answer, as I knew I must not, even to save my own skin. Feigning irritation expertly, he then tossed a thick book in my direction, saying, 'You will not be giving any secrets away, look in there.' The book appeared to be a complete list of RAF establishments in Great Britain, listed in alphabetical order, along with whatever unit or squadron was stationed there. He had urged me to look at it, obviously thinking it to be a trump card, but at that moment his telephone rang and he had to take his eyes off me while he answered it. Flicking quickly through the pages of the book, I was able to test its accuracy by looking for two airfields that I knew to be new. They were not listed, which gave me a little bit of satisfaction, thinking, 'He does not know everything then', but this did little to allay my fears.

The telephone call must have been more important than grilling me, for while he continued with it the guards entered and took me back to my cell, feeling that I was living on borrowed time and certainly not in the clear.

It was almost two days before I was marched off down the corridors again. I had had plenty of opportunity to wake up to the fact that even if my captors knew that I was in the same aircraft as David, it was no proof that I was a genuine crew member. As a result, I was so terrified of what I was about to encounter that I did not notice that I was being taken off in a different direction this time. It came as a surprise then, when I was ushered into a different room to face a different interrogator.

This officer presented a friendly attitude and although we had been warned many times by the RAF Intelligence to be on guard against this approach, it was a great relief when he straight away said, 'Now, we are both wireless people, technicians, so we understand each other.'

He did not question my identity at all and did not ask any questions for some time, but then, quite unexpectedly, still maintaining his friendly manner, he fired a question that stunned me. 'Were you carrying Fishpond?' he asked.

About three weeks previously, while still on the squadron, when there was to be no operations that night, all aircrew wireless operators were told to report to the Operations Room immediately. We all wondered what all this was about, as, on arrival, we could see that Service Police were there in force, guarding not only the doors, but all approaches.

It turned out we were to be introduced to, and given a demonstration of, a new piece of equipment that would not only detect and warn of the approach of another aircraft, as the current Aural Monica did, but would also show the direction it was coming from. It was to be under the control of the wireless operator who could then warn the gunners over the intercom. The new equipment was given the codename Fishpond and secrecy, we were told repeatedly, was paramount.

I was too shocked to answer immediately, but an answer was not necessary because almost in the same breath he said, 'Come with me,' and led me off to another room where Fishpond was set up and working. There he gave me my second demonstration of its qualities. Nothing else was asked or said before I was returned to my cell.

The difference in this man's attitude made me feel even more uncertain. To start with I had been accused of being an agent and now I was being asked a question that only an RAF operational wireless operator would know about.

*

Any hope I might have built up was lost when, nearly two days later, I was marched off to face my first interrogator once more. Neither his attitude nor his accusations had changed, and when I again refused to answer his questions, he said, 'Well, you offer me no alternative, I must hand you over to the Gestapo.'

Back home we had heard a lot about the Gestapo and its brutal methods, so his threat was indeed chilling. He would be aware of this, so added, 'And we all know what they will do to you, don't we?'

Deep down I still thought he was bluffing, but when I reminded myself that this man had the power to do what he liked with me, justified or not, and that there was absolutely no one to even talk to about my predicament, let alone to get help from, it was of little comfort.

Before dismissing me, he again asked about my aircrew, but accepted my refusal to answer without much pressure, which only made me think that he was not concerned if I did not want to help myself. Back in my cell I was left to stew for many more lonely hours.

Next, the wireless man sent for me again. His approach and attitude again differed greatly from his colleague and, in what appeared to be a friendly manner, he tried to get me talking about technical details. He was not very persistent, which made me suspect that he too knew I was going to the Gestapo and thought there was no point in wasting his time with me.

I was soon escorted back to the solitude of my cell.

*

In the afternoon of that day a different fear came from an unexpected source. With the sound of aircraft overhead, there came a terrible feeling that the cell was vibrating and I was about to be crushed. This was followed by the fear that all the air was being drawn out of the cell. I concluded that, although some distance away, this was a knock-on effect of hundreds of bombs being dropped at the same time, on the same place, by the Americans using their method of carpet bombing. It was terrifying.

Adding to my worries, I recalled that during the lectures which were given about this place, we were told that we would usually be kept for ten days. 'If they keep you for longer', we were told, 'be aware because you are probably telling them something or they think that you might do.' Calculating that this was my ninth day, how could I be sure that they were not getting something out of me? The complete isolation exaggerated all my problems; there had been no warning given about this in the lectures.

The next day saw another dreaded session with the espionage man, as I came to label him. His approach this time was surprisingly one of 'Let's see if we can get you off the hook'. His manner seemed to be a lot softer, when he went on to say, 'In a mortuary in Berlin, there are the bodies of six British airmen. All I ask you to do is to name them, so that graves can be marked in the proper manner.'

I knew, and I am sure he knew, that they could not all be from my aircrew. Looking back, of course this was his ploy to get me talking, but I could not see that at the time, so I was mystified, suspicious and baffled. Failing to draw me on this subject, his stern and aggressive manner returned, and he delivered what I sensed to be my final, grim warning.

'This is now a matter for the Gestapo,' he barked, whereupon the guards entered to march me back to my cell. I slumped on my bed no longer thinking that he was bluffing. There was no doubt in my mind now – I was on my way to be tortured and then shot.

*

Terror struck in the early afternoon when the unsettling sound of boots came to a smart halt outside my cell. The door was flung open and two guards stood looking at me for the final time. After what seemed to be an age one of them ordered, 'Pick up your belongings, you are leaving.'

I only had my battledress blouse to pick up, so with that in one hand, they marched me at what seemed to be a much quicker pace than usual, along the corridors. My feet felt very heavy and my knees went weak thinking, 'I am on my way to the Gestapo, first to be tortured and then shot.' Then, as we halted at a door that appeared to lead to the outside, the even more frightening thought came to me: 'They are going to shoot me now.'

When the door was flung open, however, I was pushed not into a yard with a firing squad, as I was expecting, but into a large, bright room crowded with Allied Airmen. They were laughing, talking and smoking cigarettes, creating an unmistakable atmosphere of wellbeing. My sense of relief was indescribable. I was not to be shot. My interrogation was over, and I was amongst the boys again. Then I was greeted by the rather splendid sight of David coming towards me with his usual grin at its best.

I think I was the last prisoner to join the group and soon learned that they had already been told that they would be leaving for a prison camp that day.

We must have been a very sorry looking bunch gathered there. Several, like David and I, were bandaged up and some were limping rather badly. We all looked very dirty, as there had been no washing facilities during our incarceration and nearly two weeks of grime had been added to the bloodstains and bruises, but we were well aware then, and will never forget, that we were the lucky ones.

In an adjoining room we were pleasantly surprised to find some food had been set out for us; nothing exotic: biscuits, cheese, tinned meat and a delicious fruit drink, but it tasted so nice after the sour black bread and swede soup. The meal was not down to the generosity or compassion of our captors but had come from Red Cross parcels and was set out by a work party of British POWs who were held at Dulag Luft. Looking back, I think this could have been allowed and encouraged by the Germans in the hope that we would be put off guard and forget about the hidden microphones we had been warned about, and divulge some information they were looking for, but I cannot remember any talk at all; not out of a sense of duty, but because all interest was centred on the food, which all went far too quickly.

After this brief and unexpected treat, we were each handed another. The American Red Cross had provided an attaché case which, although made of cardboard, was very strong and contained a towel, soap, a toothbrush and paste and some shaving gear. These items were of no immediate use without water but were very much appreciated and were to become treasured possessions in POW life.

Also available, for those in need, were boots from the Canadian Red Cross. The boots I had been provided with at Tempelhof airfield – you may recall I had somehow lost one of my own in the air – had a very cold and unfriendly feel to them and I was glad to discard them for a pair of soft, warm and comfortable Royal Canadian Airforce ones. We were always told how methodical the Germans were with their records, but unbelievably, almost before I had taken the borrowed boots off, a Luftwaffe airman appeared, scooped them up, gave them a brief inspection and marched off with them. I must have been a marked prisoner from the moment I put them on. I hope he recorded their return or I might yet get a bill for them.

All flying clothing had been confiscated (those who had managed to evade capture for a time, would have discarded and hidden theirs to look as much like a civilian as possible) so it came as a pleasant surprise when RAF greatcoats were then handed out to everyone from the Red Cross store. Those coats were to become invaluable as we were destined for what was probably the most northerly Stalag for Allied prisoners, and warm clothing was something we would all need to face the cold, harsh German winter.

*

We must have looked a very strange party as we left Dulag Luft on that cold February afternoon. Dirty, ragged, bandaged and limping, but each carrying a brand-new attaché case. Unlike the journey we made coming to Frankfurt, we were not going to enjoy the comfort of travelling in passenger coaches, but neither were we going to be exposed to the very aggressive civilians. On the other hand, the guards escorting us might not be so skilled in protecting us or have reason to be, as we had all been fully interrogated now, and were of much less value to our captors.

We were quickly loaded on to waiting lorries under heavy guard and transported to a railway goods yard not far away. They stopped alongside a train made up of goods wagons which instantly reminded me of those shown on the Pathé Newsreel, at my local Odeon cinema earlier in the war, taking Jews off to detention camps. Nobody then, outside Germany, could guess what their terrible fate would be; at least in that respect I was spared apprehension.

RAF Intelligence had warned us of a ploy that might be used at Dulag Luft. In return for answers to their questions, they would offer a quick transfer to a POW camp, where the accommodation would be very comfortable, with adequate sports facilities and all the comforts of modern life. No doubt the poor Jewish people were deceived in a similar fashion in the earlier days to make the task of transporting them to their deaths a little easier for their evil captors. Later in the war they were brutally and unashamedly forced into them. I have never understood how the Nazis were able to conceal their crimes against the Jews from the rest of the world for so long. I suppose it had a lot to do with the truth being so unimaginable, no one would have suspected it.

Our guards remained very efficient and quickly got all our party transferred into one of the rail wagons, leaving not the slightest chance of any of us slipping away into the gathering darkness. Once inside it could be seen that security had been well taken care of with the interior divided into three sections by heavy timber and barbed wire. The centre section, where there was a sliding door on each side for loading purposes, was occupied by three or four armed guards. We were detained in the two end sections, with only a narrow door, securely bolted from the centre section, being the only possible means of escape.

The friendly company of other Allied airmen was a vast improvement on the loneliness and anxiety of Dulag Luft and although there was not enough room for each prisoner to lie down on the floor of the wagon, there was just enough room, while sitting upright along each side, to straighten our legs. Little did I realise that this was a relative luxury and, as the journey was only going to take a day or two, far worse journeys were to come during my long captivity.

We could see the guards through the barbed wire preparing their evening meal. Nothing we would envy at that time – a piece of black sausage and a hunk of black bread – but a few months later the sight of anything edible, just out of reach, would have been a torment. They also had a small coal burning stove, which they used to make a hot drink, that ersatz coffee, but the heat output of the stove would have been too small to make any noticeable difference to the very cold temperatures that had to be endured by all.

The night soon passed with several stops being made. With each stop we thought our journey was completed, but as it became daylight the reason for the stops became clear – our train had no priority and was frequently put into a siding to allow other trains to pass. As it got slightly warmer the guards slid one of the doors open a crack, and apart from being grateful for the fresh air, it allowed some view of what was going on outside and told us that we were travelling north, towards the Russian Front.

While waiting patiently in yet another siding, it could be seen that trains passing in our direction were made up of flat platform trucks carrying field guns and lorries, while trains going in the opposite direction were mainly hospital trains. Soldiers could be seen standing at the windows, mostly with their heads bandaged, or with one or even both arms in slings, but looking quite cheerful – supposedly only too glad to get away from a terrible war. In other carriages the seriously wounded could be seen lying on stretchers. Although they were the enemy it was still shocking to see them in such a condition.

Chapter 4

Stalag Luft VI

At some stage, towards the end of the second night, our train came to a halt and, in the growing light, the guards could be seen putting on their packs and gathering up their rifles. We had arrived.

One of the doors was slid fully open and we were ordered out. The guards, who had been considerably strengthened by a detail from the prison camp, formed us up, much as we would have been in the square-bashing days of the RAF, and marched us off.

It was not a long or arduous march, perhaps even enjoyable after the confinement of the cattle truck, but upon arriving at our destination, our spirits took a nose dive as we surveyed Stalag Luft VI.

Originally built at the start of the war near the town of Heydekrug to house Polish prisoners, it was the northernmost POW camp within the confines of the German Reich. As Nazi aggression swept Europe, POWs from France and Belgium were added, followed by Russians. June 1943 saw a new clientele made up of British and Canadian Air Force non-commissioned officers, and, from February 1944, they were joined by American airmen unfortunate enough to be captured. By July 1944 it housed nine thousand Allied airmen.

On seeing it for the first time my attention was immediately taken by the amount of barbed wire involved. It not only surrounded the Stalag entirely and very securely, but within that were separate areas known as lagers or compounds (at Stalag Luft VI there were three: A, E and K), which were just as securely fenced from each other, creating prisons within a prison.

The fences, it seemed, were erected to a standard pattern, for wherever I went they all looked alike. There was, in fact, always two fences running parallel, about twelve feet apart, and about the same in height, thickly stranded with barbed wire, with the gap between them filled entirely with coiled barbed wire. The posts were of natural, unmachined, substantial tree trunks. As would be expected, the defences extended well below ground level.

At each corner of the wired-off areas were watch towers, referred to as Posten boxes. These were platforms hoisted a further ten feet above wire on timber stilts with a roof. They provided the guards who manned them, day and night, an uninterrupted view of both sides of the fences. The guards were armed with mounted machine guns and rifles, and for night use, searchlights to supplement the overhead lighting around the wire barriers.

Perhaps twenty feet from the wire, which all the boundary fences were known as by the prisoners, and on the inside, ran the warning wire. This was quite insignificant in appearance but the strict rule, laid down by our captors, was if any prisoner so much as touched it, they would be considered as attempting to escape and shot without further warning. This rule had to be accepted, and no one in their right mind would ever put it to the test.

When I look back, in my old age, I realise how easy it would have been for a prisoner to accidentally fall on to that low to the ground warning wire, for just inside of it, around the entire boundary of each compound, was a well-trodden path known as the circuit. This gave the longest uninterrupted walk possible, and it was very popular with most prisoners, in all weathers. Apart from the fresh air, which was so welcome after being shut up in a very crowded hut for many hours, if there was anything to discuss about RAF matters, escape plans or anything that our captors must not know about, this was the only place where there could not be any hidden microphones, or the enemy not secretly listening. It became crowded at times, especially on a fine day, and the chances of someone stumbling and accidentally touching the wire, was certainly not impossible.

*

Our party was marched from the main gate through several internal, but no less well guarded gates, to E Lager, which was very obviously newly opened and almost entirely occupied by American airmen. We were then herded into a large and, for a short time only, not overcrowded hut. There were no Americans in this hut but although we were segregated by huts, we could mix with them freely otherwise, and it was to be a very interesting experience.

The Americans were friendly, helpful and interesting, but I found them a little surprising. It must be remembered that there were no transatlantic air services in my youth; even if there had been the average person of that day would not have had the leisure time or the money to use them, and the same applied to the luxury sea crossings that were available. Knowledge of Americans came from the films that were shown at the local cinemas – most popular before the days of television. I would say ninety-five per cent of films shown were American, so we thought we really knew all about them. Those living in the cities were all well off – they took their girls out to dinner driving big cars or hailed a cab by clicking a finger and thumb, and there was always one at hand, or they were cowboys. These were quite different and spent most of their time at war with the Red Indians, showing unbelievable accuracy with their six shooters and always winning. In their spare time they would demonstrate their other skill, that of lassoing cattle.

The surprise was that they were much like us; back home they did ordinary jobs to earn an ordinary living. They were perhaps, in general, a bit more extrovert, especially when playing sports. We soon learned to play softball with them and had to get used to what we thought was the ungentlemanly barracking that went on, to try to put the striker off his game.

It was not long before American airmen were wearing RAF battledress blouses and vice versa. I did not swap mine as I thought the RAF ones looked warmer and more suitable for the bitter cold Baltic weather.

On the subject of clothing, heavy, warm clothing was an absolute necessity for all the crew of a Lancaster flying at high altitudes, except for the wireless operator. This was due, in my humble opinion, to a fault in an otherwise very well-designed aircraft, namely the heating system. Hot air was ducted from one of the engines on the port side to enter the aircraft close to the wireless operator's feet, but there was no provision for the distribution of the heat once inside the aircraft. The navigator, who sat very close to me, got very little benefit from the system and the pilot, engineer and bomb aimer, none at all. It was designed so the two gunners had to rely on their electrically heated clothing, which was inadequate for the temperatures often encountered, while the heat being poured in at the wireless operator's feet was sometimes almost unbearable and could lead him into a dangerous complacency as he dressed accordingly. He would wear only his ordinary battledress uniform, and over that the essential safety equipment. A May West life jacket and parachute harness of course had to be worn. A flying helmet was always worn because it contained the oxygen mask, earphones and microphone. Flying boots were worn as a protection from the uncomfortable heat, not the cold.

We had been reminded and warned of complacency by our Wing Commander at the briefing for our raid. When referring to the general details he said, 'And you wireless operators take note – you might think you will always be snug and warm in your position, but if you get a bit of Perspex knocked out, you will know all about it. At least take your white sweater with you...' which I did, '...even if you do not wear it, take it with you and stow it where you can get at it quickly'.

Immediately upon being attacked, when the cockpit roof was badly damaged, the wisdom of his words was brought home to me. Even in all the panic and shock I was very much aware of the unbelievably instant and severe drop in temperature. If our aircraft had survived that attack, would I have survived the return flight of three or four hours? At best, I think I would have suffered badly from frostbite.

*

The white sweater was a popular issue of flying clothing that, being heavily knitted in pure wool, was very warm and had an added quality. Because it was not obviously military in appearance, and even when worn with uniform trousers, it might help an airman shot down in enemy territory look less conspicuous when trying to evade capture.

Resistance groups in France, Belgium and Holland were aware of the white sweater. RAF Intelligence had told us that if contact was made with a Resistance Group, one of the tests they might carry out to make sure that you were genuine RAF and not an enemy agent planted in the chain, was to pluck a strand of the yarn from the sweater and offer it to a flame. If it only smouldered, this would show that the garment was made of pure wool and probably genuine. If the sample flared up, it was a synthetic material and the garment not a genuine RAF issue. No doubt the Resistance would soon be made aware that the Germans were now confiscating the genuine article, so the test would be of no value.

*

While walking the circuit one afternoon, two guards armed with rifles and fixed bayonets could be seen escorting a boy, dressed in knickerbocker trousers and a tweed jacket, through the main gate into our lager. The boy wore a foreign looking peaked cap and was grinning in an arrogant and defiant way. He looked far too young to be joining us but was marched straight into one of the American huts. It was a week or so before I learned the story behind this boy's arrival.

It turned out that the boy really was an American airman. During a raid on Germany several months before, his aircraft, a B29, was shot down over France. He managed to evade immediate capture and was given shelter by a French family, at great risk to themselves. He was not passed on to a resistance group, as we had always been told would happen, but kept by the family as one of them. He lived quite openly it seemed, even occasionally doing a newspaper delivery job in full daylight, going to the barber's shop for a haircut several times and generally living a normal life. His ability to do this would have been down to, firstly, the support given by a very brave family (I was not told what happened to them but they could have been shot) and, secondly, his remarkable physical appearance. It came as no surprise to find that the new prisoner was a ball man, which meant that he would have manned the ball-shaped gun turret protruding below the belly of the B29; to be able to even get into one, a man needs to be short in stature and slim.

Another interesting character, who came to join our ranks, was a Frenchman called Maurice who arrived two or three days after David and I. He could speak English very well and gradually, bit by bit, we heard the most incredible story. At the outbreak of the war, in 1939, Maurice was too young for military service, but after the fall of France, in 1940, he became involved with the Resistance Movement. He was mainly tasked with helping Allied soldiers and airmen evade capture and get to Britain, where they could join up with their old units. He then escaped to Britain himself, in a very small boat, where he joined the RAF and became a fighter pilot. On an offensive sweep over France he was shot down but survived uninjured to re-join the Resistance. Some time later he was arrested during a Gestapo raid but was able to prove, because he had time to put on his uniform and was already wearing his identity discs, that he was RAF and, therefore, a prisoner of war according to the Geneva Convention.

*

Our hut soon reached capacity and we had to get used to the way of life inside a prisoner of war camp. The most common type of huts, I was never in any other, were built together, rather like a row of terraced houses, but they only had a ground floor. To maximise space the beds were either two or three tier bunks, lined up on each of the side walls, and placed so close together it was a tight squeeze to get into them. This arrangement allowed around sixty prisoners to be penned up in each hut, but left little floor space for eating, cooking or any other domestic task. Fresh air was basically inadequate because there were only two small windows in the back wall and two more and the door at the front. Before darkness fell, the windows were shuttered up and the door securely bolted from the outside. I shudder to think what the air quality must have been at the end of a long winter night. In very warm weather there was a concession, the windows were left uncluttered allowing a bit more ventilation, but any attempt to even lean out of them would be risking a fierce attack by a guard dog or being shot by a patrolling guard.

There were no washing facilities in the huts and the lavatory for night use was a large metal drum which had to be emptied each morning into a pit near to the main latrine block, some distance away. The transporting of it, and it was quite heavy, was made possible by the provision of two wooden poles, which could be passed through a bracket on each side of the drum, with a man front and rear. I suppose it was like carrying a Sedan Chair with a different sort of passenger. The task was done on a rota basis with the two-man team excused all other hut fatigues, so it had its good side.

There was never any running water provided in the huts. In the place where we washed, water had to be pumped up by a semi-rotary hand pump. This was done on a rota system, each hut in turn, providing a succession of pumpers on its pumping days.

Red Cross food parcels were regularly available when we first arrived at Stalag Luft VI, and I cannot emphasise enough what a lifesaver they were. Even with them, we always felt hungry, but we were not starving. They were issued based on one parcel per man per week. Each one was opened under the scrutiny of the Germans, which was understandable, and any tins of food were not allowed to be taken away without first being punctured, as they would be very useful for escape purposes.

Our staple diet consisted of a meagre potato ration which was cooked in a communal kitchen. These were never peeled, in order to maintain what little nutritional value they had, and, psychologically, this was comforting as the skin took a little longer to chew. The contents of Red Cross tins were added to the potato ration to make corned beef hash or salmon clop, which was popular because it added a bit of bulk which was sorely needed.

There was only one small stove in each hut, and even that had a totally inadequate fuel supply, so individual cooking was limited to making toast with one of the precious slices of bread, if you had enough patience, and even then this was not recommended by the British Medical Officer, warning that the toasting of bread destroyed some of its nutritional value.

After a week or so in the prison camp the German bread, previously despised, took on a new image as hunger really set in, and it became craved.

The daily ration was issued firstly to the communal kitchen on the strict basis of one loaf to seven men, and from there to the huts, and it was here that the unenviable task of cutting each loaf into seven equal parts, before an audience of very hungry Krieges (an abbreviation of the long German name, Kriegsgefangene, meaning prisoner of war), was undertaken. It was carried out by a volunteer who had been a grocer and provision merchant in civilian life; although I am ashamed to admit I did not appreciate the value of his work at the time. The loaf was not uniform in shape and although of a standard weight, we had no scales to help decide what was a fair seventh, so it all depended on his skilled hand and eye coordination. During the cutting process if a crumb of the bread fell from the table it never reached the floor – there were too many hungry bystanders with eye and hand finely tuned to snap up this rare minute treat.

The temptation of eating it all as soon as it arrived was, on the advice of more experienced Krieges, resisted, but it took strong willpower and the experience of the long wait for the next issue to see the wisdom of this.

Also prepared daily and distributed by the communal kitchen was the midday soup which was no more than boiled swede. It was brought to each hut in a wooden tub and as another permanent fatigue, one man had the job of ladling this out to everyone in the hut. This was easier to share out than the bread because each man's share could be measured using a skilled eye and hand with the ladle and making sure the watery soup was stirred frequently to distribute the lumps of swede. The only differential in the portions was that the splinters of wood that came from the tub became much more evident towards the bottom, and it was an acquired skill to separate the swede from the wood before spitting out.

It is no surprise to learn I was around twelve stone when I was captured but over the course on my internment I, like everyone else, lost a lot of weight – and strength, we didn't want to do much at all but lay on the bunks – and was only around nine stone coming out; we were like skeletons.

*

We were forever on edge, living with the fear of what may happen next. There was one alarming incident, early on, that demonstrates this perfectly. One afternoon, without warning, two guards came into our hut armed with rifles and bayonets. They were accompanied by one of the security guards known as ferrets, who were always to be treated with suspicion as despite their seemingly innocent 'just passing by' attitude, they were very much on the lookout for any illegal activities or possessions. On this occasion there was just one single purpose – he had come to take the Frenchman away for further questioning.

Maurice looked terrible, but there was nothing any of us could have done to help, as he was marched out between the guards, while the ferret searched his pitiful left-behind possessions. Happily, we did hear later that he had been returned to the camp after this ordeal.

Our Camp Leader or Man of Confidence, to use his official title, was aware of what had happened and demanded to speak to the Camp Commandant. It was said that he got full co-operation from him (it was no secret that the ordinary German military had no love for the Gestapo or the SS), which was not surprising to anyone who knew him.

*

James 'Dixie' Deans, a Scottish bomber pilot who was shot down in 1940, spoke perfect German and became a renowned prisoner of war camp leader. He was eventually awarded the MBE and became a founder member and first president of the RAF Ex-POW Association. In 1945, he was to guide two thousand Allied POWs across Europe in what was known as the Long March, but more on that later.

Deans had the absolute trust and admiration of all the prisoners. He had that rare quality of being able to get respect from all, and yet he never shouted or threatened. He was always calm and collected and knew just how far to push the Germans and be uncooperative without risking a mass execution of those under his leadership, and yet he still earned and maintained the respect of our captors. I will never forget him or cease to be eternally grateful that he was there to guide and protect us.

Chapter 5

Life behind the wire

The course of one's life can be greatly altered by a single event and, although I had no idea at the time, there soon occurred one such instance in which fate was, once more, to be kind to me and make a significant difference in the way I was treated in my POW life.

The Germans had decided to shake things up a bit and we were told by the guards to pack up our meagre possessions as we were to be moved across to K lager. While David and I were not moved into the same hut this time, he was placed in a hut just opposite; we were still in close and easy contact.

Settling into my new hut I could see distinct signs of more organisation, which was understandable because most of the prisoners there had been in captivity for considerably longer than us new arrivals. They were very welcoming, and I was invited to join a long-established group of five who always sat at the same table and to some extent shared things, but not food. This was always individual as it was so precious.

Interestingly two of the group or combine, as each

group was known, were from my squadron. They had both been in the Bag, as our internment was sometimes referred to, for around two years. I had to bide my time to catch up on old times as talk of the squadron was only safe when walking the circuit.

The first example of organisation in K Lager came on my first day there, when a smartly dressed man wearing collar and tie, which was a rare sight, entered the hut. He was obviously well known to all but me, and they knew what he had come for. Simultaneously space was cleared for him at one of the tables. A man was posted on each of the windows and the door was closed, and all went quiet. In a cultured voice, very similar to that of a BBC announcer, he spoke out, 'This is the news in English', and he went on to read from a sheet which contained, what we would call today, news headlines.

A little trick that the newsreader had at hand, I heard about later, was that if a ferret came into the hut during the reading, he had at the ready a copy of the German news bulletin, and he would switch quickly to this, which was perfectly legal.

Although this service, which sometimes took place twice a day, was eagerly anticipated and greatly appreciated, it could dampen the spirits a touch as the progress of the war appeared to be very slow or static at times. We were impatient waiting for the day when soldiers would come, break down the gates and set us free. It wasn't until some time after the war was over that it was revealed what a bitter and courageous struggle the armies had made to make the progress they did, on all fronts, and we realised how even more grateful we should all have been for their sacrifices. I think the media, as it is called today, tended to emphasise the good bits and not tell of the bad. Perhaps they were made to do this to boost morale at home, however, I will tell later of one instance where this policy did not go down well with those fighting the war right at the front.

Very shortly after being moved to K Lager all new arrivals were instructed by their various hut leaders to attend a meeting. No reason was given, we were just told to be there. It turned out we were to be seen individually by a panel of much-respected old timers from A lager. Some of these claimed they had been in Germany longer than many millions of Germans, which I suppose was true, but they were not rewarded for that. They had earned respect for being clever, reliable people who had assisted the Camp Leader in his arduous work whenever needed.

It came as a shock when my turn came to take up the seat in front of them, to realise that I was being interrogated by them to ascertain whether I was genuine RAF or not; I soon saw the sense in what they had done.

My identity verified, they wanted to know all I had seen during the journey from Dulag Luft, especially the rail traffic. One or two questions about what I was asked at Dulag Luft followed and then I was thanked, reminded to keep my trap shut, then, with a wink and a smile, dismissed. I had more sense than to ask what it was all for. I never imagined that in about a year, in a very humble way, and only for about two weeks, I would be helping in this sort of work.

*

While it didn't do to dwell on such matters for too long, thoughts did drift back home to your loved ones. Our only contact was by letter, but such luxuries were few and far between. Prisoners could write a lettercard home once a month. It was known by us that this would be heavily censored before leaving Germany, so it was difficult to know what would be allowed through. Likewise, we could receive one letter a month.

I had found myself thinking about Adelaide quite a lot, as you can imagine – I later learnt that she did not receive news that I was still alive, inside a prisoner of war camp, until quite a while after I had been shot down. I would always be excited on the rare occasion a letter got through but, for whatever reason, we only received one or two letters from each other during the whole time. I was extremely glad to get the first and pleased to know that she was still thinking of me and hadn't written me off.

Sadly, that happened quite a lot, even married chaps had news come through that their wives had gone off with somebody else. They were referred to as Dear John letters; I think the term originated from the POW camps. They were devastated. You have nothing and then that letter arrives. They just had to cope with it; like a lot of other things. You tried to help them along but some of them took on a bitter attitude. It must have been terrible news for them.

I can remember another letter from Adelaide's younger sister, Barbara, which gave me some idea what was happening back at Husbands Bosworth. Although only twelve-years-old she managed to conceal meaning in her 'innocent' letter. I guessed that her words 'It's all quiet on the Sulby Road as usual', must surely mean the opposite and that meant the Wellingtons must still be roaring overhead and the Drome was still training aircrew. I knew that, ever since the Drome was opened, the aircraft noise on Sulby Road was continuous and deafening and therefore it could not possibly be 'usual' for it to be quiet. This was a small, but welcome psychological boost for someone isolated from Churchill's battle roar.

*

Prisoners were also allowed a personal parcel. I think this was only every three months, and even that was not maintained – not because they were not sent out by relatives regularly, but they did not arrive. While the Germans were not suspected of pilfering them – they were quite honourable in some things – the parcels came indirectly, via a neutral country, so it would be difficult to say where or how they went astray.

Cigarette parcels, which could be sent more frequently, fared even worse. They too came indirectly, but, being smaller, were probably easier to pilfer. You might say now, knowing about the dangers of smoking, that was a good thing, but in those days we were led to believe that smoking was good for you, as it calmed the nerves and helped a person think more clearly, and that it was a great social asset. Consequently, probably nine out of ten men smoked, including me, and quite a lot of women. In a prison camp, cigarettes took on a whole new dimension, they were currency, so the few non-smokers and the lucky ones who fared a bit better with their cigarette parcels, such as the Canadians, could buy things from other prisoners. I must say at this point, the Canadians were always generous to their hut mates and I enjoyed many a packet of Sweet Caporal cigarettes; they were a great morale booster when times were especially bad.

Cigarettes could be earned in the more prosperous times by a few prisoners who were talented in drawing and, by using a photograph as a guide, could produce a portrait in pencil. Some were remarkably talented and I sometimes wonder if any of them ever became professional artists later in life. The number of items that were bought and sold for cigarettes was never large and became almost non-existent as 1944 wore on, when even the Canadian parcels were not coming through.

Bread was never on sale within the camp – that was priceless – but there were contacts from outside where a loaf could be bought. I did hear that one of the guards was involved, but it would have been pointless trying to find out more without having the means to carry the deal through, and it was also very risky.

It was years after my POW days before it occurred to me what a lot of clever work was done by our Camp Leader and his aides in obtaining items and the services of people from the outside. It all had to be thought through very carefully because of the risk of counter intelligence. For example, maintaining the secret radio would require a supply of spare parts and batteries, but if the wrong person was contacted to supply them it could get back to the Germans which would confirm that there was a radio in the camp and probably reveal its hiding place.

Many things would have to be secretly obtained towards an organised escape bid – clothing, train timetables and much general information about the locality. This could only have been done with bribery and the only thing these clever, dedicated people had to use for that purpose, to my knowledge, would come out of the Red Cross parcels. Cigarettes, chocolate and real coffee I imagine would be very tempting to the Germans as they endured severe austerity in that sort of thing.

Perhaps some of the goods had to be first exchanged for Reichsmarks before the objective could be achieved. Whatever had to be done was for the good of us all, and this group of courageous people, the Escape Committee, the name they were known by in all Stalag Lufts, should have had special recognition when they returned home to their various countries; I don't think they did.

*

I had been in K6 some weeks, when at around 5am, guards burst into the hut and ordered everyone out. That meant dressed in whatever we usually slept in. It was still very cold at that time of the morning, despite the improving temperatures by day, and we were kept standing there for some considerable time. It would become obvious in a short while that others in the hut had guessed what this was all about, but nothing was said. Eventually we were ordered back inside the hut. I happened to be one of the first back in, so got a front seat you might say, to see all that took place.

Right in the lead, with his own personal guard, was Jock, our Room Leader, and he was escorted into the small room where the night latrine was housed. Jock, like the Camp Leader, did not have to shout to make sure everybody knew he was in charge. He was a quiet mannered Scot, who on first acquaintance might appear dour, but look more carefully and there was always a hint of humour in his eyes. He did everything quietly and efficiently and was accepted by all without question.

I could see when I got to the door of the latrine room that nearly all the space was taken up by a group of sinister looking civilians. I immediately thought, 'These are Gestapo', as they were dressed in long black overcoats, trilby hats, with the brim turned down front and back, and leather jack boots. Although concealed, a bulge in their coats revealed that they were armed with pistols; they appeared almost exactly like the Gestapo were portrayed in the films shown at my local cinema back home.

The latrine drum had been pushed to one side and a paving slab had been removed to reveal a neat hole, a bit smaller in area than the slab. It was obviously a shaft leading to a tunnel below. I had no knowledge of the tunnel, but I hadn't long joined the hut and those working on it would never have told of its existence because they weren't really sure who I was; I could have been a German plant for all they knew.

Jock had been hustled into a position by his escort to stand on one side of the shaft so that he was facing a man who must have been the senior Gestapo officer. The German took his time to stare at Jock before he almost screamed out the question, 'And what is the meaning of this?' thrusting a finger at the hole. Jock, unaffected by his attitude, did nothing for what seemed an age, and just stood and stared into the hole feigning surprise and disbelief. Next, Jock moved around the hole 90 degrees, and from his new position, stood with a puzzled look studying the hole with disbelief, for what seemed another age of time. The Gestapo man became even angrier, made visible by his face becoming redder by the second, until it seemed he was about to explode.

We all wondered what Jock's next move would be because he could not play this out much longer. He was now standing almost at the side of a very angry and impatient Gestapo officer, the kind who were not known for their kindness to prisoners. Jock now moved slowly and thoughtfully to the opposite side of the shaft once more and looked into the hole again. Eventually, when he was ready, he scratched his head, then turned to the officer and, with his face the picture of innocence, said, 'Well look at that, rats.'

The Gestapo officer exploded. He threw his arms in the air and his whole body went up with both feet well clear of the ground. He was barely in control of himself. Spitting and fuming as he did so, he screamed back, 'Rats? Rats? Do you think we are stupid?' Then, without waiting for Jock's answer, he motioned to the guard who had escorted Jock in, shouting, 'Cooler.' The guard sprang to attention and off they went with Jock giving one of his rare smiles.

The Cooler was the name given to the detention centre or punishment cells where sentences for misbehaviour were served. Usual punishment would vary between one and fourteen days according to the seriousness of the misbehaviour. Jock was given, I think, four days by the Camp Commandant, which was lenient. Perhaps it was his way of 'getting back' at the Gestapo. Even so, the Cooler was not a pleasant place to be in – absolute solitude and the food was even more sparse than usual.

*

Life went on in K Lager and we were always hungry, sometimes very hungry. While it seemed that there was no change in the progress of the war, prisoners kept each other going morale wise. There was often someone ready to throw himself at the wire and make an end to it, but luckily there was always a friend who would boost his spirits enough to prevent this.

There was one prisoner who would tantalise those around him, usually just before they were about to get to sleep, by saying loudly what he was going to have for breakfast on the first morning he got home again. He would reel off a mouth-watering menu of eggs, bacon, sausage, mushrooms, tomatoes, black pudding and lashings of hot buttered toast, accompanied by hot sweet tea or coffee with real milk and plenty of sugar. He would then start to say what he would have to follow, but would always be shouted down, or have something thrown at him. Only those who have been very hungry for a long time would appreciate his cruel humour, but it always finished with a laugh, so it must have done a bit of good and it was only what everyone thought, often.

*

As the weather got a bit warmer life became a little easier because the mud dried up and a walk round the circuit became more enjoyable. The distant pine trees surrounding the camp appeared a little less mournful and forbidding, but the craving for food continued.

*

June 6, 1944, started as a miserable day, dull and windy, and the secret radio bulletin had told us it was Derby Day in Great Britain. Some of those more interested in horse racing had organised a simulation of the race out on the parade ground; a bit like a huge Ludo game scratched out on the ground. Punters could lay bets in cigarettes with self-appointed bookmakers, but the race never finished.

As the race progressed some very, very important and breath-taking news began spreading amongst the POWs – the Allies had landed in Normandy that morning.

It was only after the news had been posted on the official German notice board, and individuals read the notice twice over to make sure they had read it right, and then raced back to their huts, that the news was spread. As it did so, cheer after cheer rang out from some, while others hid their faces and just cried.

That dramatic news was contained in one first sentence of the German notice, and then it went on to claim that this was just what they had been waiting for. At last the Allies had delivered themselves to them, and now a pincer movement would be applied and those invaders who had not been wiped out would be driven back into the sea. This claim was not even discussed by us POWs to my knowledge. As far as we were concerned, the Allies had landed and that was that. The wonderful, almost unbelievable, news was confirmed when a BBC bulletin was read out in each hut at midday. With such an optimistic account of the progress that had been made, even the most pessimistic were now speculating on when we would be freed. Little did we know of what was to come – that it would take far longer than we could anticipate and that for too many, liberation never came, while thousands had to suffer terrible hardship before they were returned to their beloved homelands.

*

As a week or so went by, with no significant advance from the beachheads, a feeling of anti-climax began to set in. We were not made aware of the bitter battles our armies were fighting in attempting to take the city of Caen, or we would have been much more grateful for what they were achieving and prepared to wait in our comparative safety. However, as the weeks wore on, even the most pessimistic were asking, 'Will it be next week or the week after when the British Liberation Army will smash down the gates to set us free?'

*

At some point in July 1944 we noticed an obvious change in morale amongst the Germans who were guarding us, which I believe was shared by all German forces, wherever they were serving, and probably all German citizens as well. This followed the attempted assassination of Hitler in East Prussia, which could not have been that far from our Stalag in the north of the country.

The first sign of change was at morning roll call when at its completion our leader saluted the German officer in charge as normal, but this was not returned, as it always was, with a similar salute, but with a salute that everyone knew to be the Nazi one; the right arm and hand was stretched fully forward and slightly raised. It seemed that Hitler had called all his ordinary, purely military personnel, to heel, and reminded them who was boss. (What we did not know then was that control of the Allied prisoner of war camps was handed over to the SS commander, Himmler, following the assassination attempt.)

The new salute, however, was a mere detail of the change and thankfully the guards were not more aggressive to the prisoners; whatever had been inflicted on them was not to be passed on to us. It seemed, if anything, that it was to be kept secret.

From then on, the ordinary salute was not seen to be used by any German, but some of the fear that we guessed they were under – that of being posted to the Russian Front – gradually came to light. Some of our guards had already been there and, quite unofficially of course, being sure they could not be overheard, would disclose some of the horrors they had been through there. They declared that the Russians were not like British or German soldiers – they were 'animals' and did not care how many of them were killed in gaining an inch of ground.

Knowing this, but not risking a blow from a rifle butt by saying it to anyone but a guard known to be a bit amiable, who would accept a bit of teasing, prisoners might ask, looking very serious, 'Russian front, Herr Smitt?' They knew what his self-comforting answer would be – 'Nein. Nein. Too old', but we noticed that some of the old guards did disappear, very noticeably the German Warrant Officer.

He was a very firm man, but fair, and we knew what to do and what not to do when he was about. He was not a Nazi, but a true professional regular soldier. We felt safe with him, so although it might sound strange, we thought we had suffered a loss.

When the true horrors of the Concentration Camps were revealed in April 1945, ordinary Germans claimed to have no knowledge of the Gas Chambers or the primitive barbaric burning of the bodies. However, just after the attempted assassination of Hitler – remember that was in July 1944 – a new phrase began to circulate around the camp – 'If you do not behave, you will go up the chimney.' This was not used by the guards as a new threat to us but, I imagine, it was a thing that they themselves had been threatened with to tighten the newly imposed discipline.

I couldn't help but wonder: if we, in a prison camp had got to hear it, then it was hardly unbelievable that the saying, and its sinister meaning, would not be known to most of the German population.

*

Another sign that gave us some measure of hope came late one afternoon as a Dornier 217 flew over very low, and it was obvious that it was in serious trouble. One engine appeared quite dead and the other was sputtering badly. Before it had passed out of sight, four parachutes opened, so it seemed the whole crew had been saved. All the prisoners watching immediately started cheering loudly, but they were also making rude gestures. This was because they were not at all bothered about the safety of the crew, but they had seen an enemy aircraft crash. The Commandant, however, had seen the incident from a different point of view. The next morning, he had it announced at roll call that he very much appreciated the sporting spirit shown by the British airmen when the German airmen were able to escape with their lives. He meant well.

Around this time, I was to get some welcome news of a different kind. Quite by chance, I was talking to a fellow prisoner who was also an airman in Bomber Command, when it became apparent that he knew that my old love rival's plane had also been shot down over Germany and that he had probably been taken prisoner. While I obviously felt sorry for him, on another level I was quietly pleased that my rival in love was also 'behind the wire' in a German Prisoner of War Camp.

*

Our thoughts of when we were going to be liberated by the British or American forces coming from the west or the south were fuelled by the belief that we could hear heavy gunfire coming from the east. Within two days we were sure there was no mistake – it was much louder and more intense. The coming of the Russians was confirmed when we could see, in the far distance, columns of civilians struggling along a road pushing handcarts and carrying all sorts of possessions. We had seen similar scenes on the newsreels at the cinema when the Germans were pushing their way across Belgium and France in 1940, so knew they were fleeing the oncoming Russians.

Everyone believed that our liberation was imminent. Amateur strategists amongst us predicted, 'they will not bother getting us out, they will only think of themselves; East Prussia is part of Germany, you see.' Even the pessimists thought they were right. We were not able to find out at that time because two days later we were all on the move.

John Martin in his RAF uniform,
aged twenty-one

Adelaide, aged eighteen,
in her WAAF uniform

Bob Brown, Mid-Upper Gunner

David Alletson, Flight Engineer

John and Adelaide's wedding, 1945

John Martin in uniform, back row centre

John and Adelaide, 2018

John Martin, 2018

John's War Medals (left to right): 1939-45 Star and medal ribbon with clasp; Air Crew Europe Star; General Service Medal

Top: Prisoner of War identity tag; second row centre: Brevet – official wireless operator's badge; second row right: Caterpillar Club membership card and badge; bottom row: John's war medals

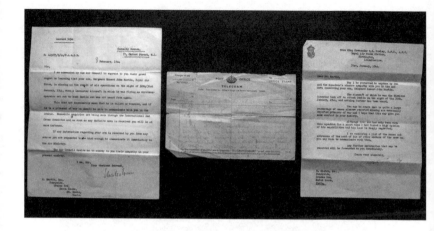

Right and left: Two letters from the Air Ministry informing John's family that his plane was shot down; centre: the initial telegram giving the news.

(Telegram reads:

31st January, 1944, 2.05pm

Regret to inform you that your son Ernest John Martin is reported missing as the result of air operations on the night of 30th Jan '44 (stop) Letter follows (stop) Any further information received will be immediately communicated to you (stop) Pending receipt of written notification from the air ministry)

Chapter 6

On the move

The evacuation of Stalag Luft VI was carried out, in July 1944, with no signs of panic from our captors; it was a hasty withdrawal but well organised. It wasn't until very early in the morning on the next day, after seeing the columns of refugees, that we found that the whole of E Lager, where the Americans were held, had already been moved out.

As this realisation began to sink in armed guards entered our own lager, separating the two rows of huts. By the time I realised what was going on, the occupants of the hut directly opposite, where David was, had already been ousted. I watched as they were moved out, carrying all they could manage in hastily made backpacks, but I could not catch sight of him. They were herded off, much like cattle, except that the drovers were much more plentiful and had bayonets fixed ready to discourage any slow movers. It was not long before all the huts on the opposite side were empty, creating a strange silent atmosphere along the whole row.

It was not until the war in Europe was over that I learned from David, and others who went with him, what a terrifying experience all those on their side of K Lager, along with the whole of the occupants of E Lager, had endured. I soon realised that, not for the first time, I had been blessed by fate through having been allocated a different hut.

Their destination was a prison camp, close to the shores of the Baltic, called Stalag Luft IV, near the town of Gross Tycho in the Province of Pomerania.

From Stalag Luft VI, they were marched to the railway station and loaded into cattle trucks in which they made the short journey to the port of Memel. There they were loaded onto a very decrepit, small merchant ship, the Insterburg, which was normally used for carrying coal in its two holds. After being ordered to leave the packs containing their pathetic possessions on deck, using just one single vertical ladder, they were forced below, into a filthy hold. The weather by now was very warm and the heat, accumulated in the steel hold, was almost unbearable; what they needed desperately was water.

The floor space of each of the two filthy, stinking holds was crammed to absolute capacity with hundreds of men. Those on the sides had great difficulty in maintaining a foothold because of the slope of the hull, and it was only after a lot of shuffling around that room was found for most men to sit with knees drawn up tight, but the heat and the air quality got worse, as did the desperate need for water. Eventually this was provided by lowering just one bucketful down at a time. Those waiting were only able to watch while others drank; this must have been torture.

Although it must have been known that the voyage would take sixty hours, no provision had been made for sanitation. Only a few of the hundreds that had been packed into the holds had been allowed back on deck after the ship set sail to relieve themselves; the rest were expected to make do with a bucket. This was raised up and down by a chain just as the water had been; some said the same bucket was used for both purposes. True or not, a bucket soon proved inadequate for this purpose and a bit of the precious floor space in the hold had to be given over to human waste. With practically no ventilation, the resultant stench increased the misery below.

To add even more terror, it was known to some of the RAF prisoners aboard that mine laying operations were frequently carried out in this area of the Baltic Sea, as a result every bang on the side of the ship when it collided with flotsam caused them to cringe, waiting for an explosion. Another thing that caused great concern to the few who had been allowed back on deck after setting sail, was that they could see that an E boat was following them. Were the German crew of their ship to be taken off at some point, leaving all the prisoners helpless when it was sunk by a torpedo?

Thankfully, after two and a half days the ship docked at the port at Swinemunde and its cargo transferred back into what would become very crowded cattle trucks once more, for what should have been a short journey inland, but they were kept penned up like cattle with no water overnight.

The next morning, as the doors were at last slid open, it could be seen that the guards who had brought them from Stalag Luft VI had departed and been replaced by very arrogant and aggressive members of what can be described as the Kriegsmarine's (German Navy) version of the Hitler Youth. They were each carrying a bayonet, and made it known that they intended to use the weapons by making a great display of sharpening them in full view of the prisoners.

It soon became obvious that on this final part of the terrible journey, it was the intention of those who had planned it to provoke the prisoners into making a mass escape. At intervals along the route machine gun nests could be spotted and moving along with the column was a film crew continually filming, supposedly to record the very start of what was hoped for. It was almost certain that only the strange sort of discipline, based on trust in their quiet unassuming leader, Vic Clarke, that prevented this from happening, when he sent word down the line, 'Don't try to run away out of line, that's what they want.' I would say, only someone who has been a prisoner of war would know why everybody obeyed without question.

The column, headed by a very tall German officer, had set off marching but his pace was so fast the prisoners had to run to keep up with him. The arrogant young sailors running alongside made sure they did so by slashing any stragglers with their bayonets unmercifully, and letting it be seen that they were enjoying it. David was stabbed twice in the back. He showed me the wounds after meeting up again, when the war ended, but told me how others had suffered far worse than he had. He was so modest; it was not until I read the book by John Nichol and Tony Rannell – The Last Escape – that I learned more fully of the threats, hardships, terror and suffering that were inflicted on these completely defenceless comrades of mine.

*

The remaining prisoners of K Lager and all those of A Lager were the next to be herded out after every single person was strip-searched at one table, while every item of clothing and all other possessions were examined at another. I mention this as an illustration of just how clever our clever men were, as, just twenty-four hours after arriving at the new Stalag, we were having the news from the BBC read out to us in the huts. Although the camp was already occupied, this service had never been available before, so all the equipment must have been smuggled out of Stalag Luft VI, concealed during the journey, and smuggled through another search, when we arrived. There were many speculations made as to how this was done, but no one would have been stupid enough to ask.

After revealing the horrors of David's journey, I will just say that our journey was very uncomfortable, and we were very glad when it ended. While travelling across what seemed to be endless flat countryside, the central doors of our truck were slid open, purely because the heat was almost unbearable for the guards, but this allowed us to see a little of what we were passing. Someone who was nearer to the wire barrier, who had a better view of the outside, suddenly shouted, 'Come and have a look at this kite.' A kite was RAF slang for aircraft. Craning forward, I could just see something in the sky climbing almost vertically, very fast and leaving a thick vapour trail as it continued to climb to a very high altitude. That was all we were able to see before it moved out of our field of vision. If we had known what we were looking at we would have been very concerned, but it was not until after repatriation, some nine months later, that we first heard of the terrible flying bombs and then the rocket attacks that had been rained on London. What we had seen, of course, was the V2 Rocket being launched at some stage of its development. Perhaps intentionally and very wisely, any reference to what London suffered because of them, was kept out of our BBC news bulletins.

Our slow train continued to rumble across the flat, featureless country of this part of Poland for what seemed to be weeks, but in fact it took only two days to arrive at our destination, or at least as far as the train was going to take us, and that was a place called Torun. We remained penned up in the trucks, and from what could be seen from the partly opened doors, it was quite a modern station, with white tiled walls and smart looking platform. Our guards stood close by with their bayonets fixed at the ready, apparently awaiting orders. Having been packed in with hardly enough room to sit down, we were impatient to get out and stretch our limbs.

Eventually, and then to only one truck at a time, the guards shouted, 'Out.' As much as we wanted to, we could not do this very quickly, after being cramped up for so long it was quite painful to move. After each end section had been carefully checked for being empty, a count was taken. Normally we would have made the count as difficult as possible for them, that was our duty, but being so relieved to be out of the truck, this was allowed to be done at their first attempt.

Moving along the platform to where the whole train load was being assembled, I saw a sign on a door indicating a lavatory. This time we did our duty by pleading we needed this facility, thereby causing more delay. Upon opening the door, it could immediately be seen that this was where the smart station ended. The floor was bare earth and in the middle of it was a pit about a metre square. Erected above this was a fencelike support made of rough timber, that allowed an agile or very desperate person to sit on the bottom rail and use the top rail to support the back. I had never seen such a primitive arrangement before or since. However, this was not the main attraction as opposite the door, in the wall, where in a more normal situation would be a window, was just a hole. The prisoner next to me knocked my arm, and knowing immediately what he meant, moved quickly over to it. In the second or two taken to do this I was thinking, 'We are now in Poland and might well get some help if we could escape.' Hopes were very quickly dashed as waiting there, with bayonets pointing straight at us, were two or three guards. We quickly retreated to re-join the group on the platform and trooped off to be formed up again on the road outside.

The march from the railway station to the prison camp, despite having had no sleep for two days, was comparatively pleasant after being crammed into a railway truck. At least the air was fresh, and it gave some sense of freedom not being surrounded by barbed wire, just the guards, and even they seemed to be enjoying the march.

I can't recall how far the camp was from the station, but while still in the town of Torun, or Thorn as it was also known, the column passed what I realised was a brothel, as from several windows of the upper floors of a large building several young ladies waved to us and smiled in a genuine sort of way.

Stalag XX-A, in Central Poland, was a long-established prison camp, so I suppose they knew who we were and where we were going, and being almost certainly Polish, were showing as much support as they dared. Whatever the circumstances, that was the first time since being captured that I had seen a friendly smile coming from a lady, let alone several ladies, and it felt good.

By the time we arrived at our destination it was getting dark. We were not put into huts initially, just a bare compound, but it was fully secured by the usual barbed wire and fully manned Posten boxes at each corner. Patrolling the inside was a strong force of dog handling guards, but that was all. There was little shelter; however, it was a warm night and straw had been spread over a large area. I don't think this was put down for our benefit, perhaps cattle had been kept here previously, but there was plenty of room to lie down and stretch out fully, which everyone did quite quickly, and I had one of the best night's sleep I can remember. On waking in the morning, we became aware that the ground and the straw must have been very wet as our clothing was soaked. This was soon forgotten as the sun was shining and it quickly got warm enough to dry us out. We then asked the usual, and far more important, question, 'When are we going to get our bread ration?'

Chapter 7

Stalag XX-A & Stalag 357

We were escorted into the main camp and fitted into huts where a few more could be squeezed in. I had already been separated from my old combine since prisoners, as might be expected, were not allowed personal preferences; you went where the guards directed you unless you wanted to be helped along by a rifle butt in the back.

Five or six of us new arrivals were put into a hut where senior Army NCOs had been long established. Most of them had been taken in North Africa and had been held in Italy until that country's capitulation in 1943. They had been most disappointed that they did not get their freedom when that happened, having been quickly taken over by the Germans and brought here.

We were soon on good terms with them – they could tell some good stories about their war in the desert – and, as we were comparatively new prisoners, they wanted to know what was going on back home. We were surprised to learn from some of them how badly they had been treated by the Italians as we always thought they would be a soft touch, but these were tough men, and of the two evils, they preferred the Germans.

*

Stalag XX-A was in many ways quite different from Stalag Luft VI; most notably, there was much more space to walk around in – but it was equally secure. The barbed wire was all there to the standard pattern, the guards were in the Posten boxes with machine guns at the ready, waiting for someone to so as much as touch the warning wire. The food ration was no more generous, set to bring about slow starvation, but the main difference was being with the Army, which expanded the topic of conversation by listening to their experiences, and vice versa.

The climate was warmer, which perhaps helped to reduce the craving for food a little, and we were in Poland where, even if they dare not do anything to help us, we knew the locals were on our side.

Before becoming a prison camp, we learned that this establishment was a Polish Army Officers Training Centre. There remained evidence that the Germans continued to use some of the land for training purposes, and we learned to be very careful where we walked. Most unusually, prisoners were allowed to be out of the huts until it was dusk and, taking advantage of this, a comrade and I had stayed out almost to the limit and were hurrying back to the hut before any shooting started.

Bill Frost, my companion, was a slightly built man who, as we were walking along chatting, suddenly disappeared, but it must have been a second or so before I realised I was talking to myself. Looking back, only his head could be seen protruding above the ground. What had happened was he had stepped into a hole only just big enough in diameter to take his body, but deep enough for him to fall up to his chin into the ground. Adding to his plight, the hole was partly filled with water. It was quite a struggle getting him out. We concluded when discussing his misadventure the next day, that we had been walking over land that had been used in anti-tank exercises, where a man could conceal himself in the path of an oncoming tank and as it passed over him he could attach an explosive device to the underside of it, which would explode and disable the tank when it got a safe distance away. Not a job to be envied.

Attached to, but not housed inside the camp, was a contingent of Russian prisoners who were used to do all the hard, manual jobs such as digging trenches or erecting fences. They were always under guard, and we were never allowed to have contact with them, but we could sometimes see them outside the wire at work and could observe how cruelly their guards treated them, frequently beating them about the body with their rifle butts for a trivial offence. Strangely, this did not appear to have much effect on the Russians, the blows just seemed to bounce off, and sometimes they would grin back at the guard, which would bring on even more punishment. The Russian prisoners, it seemed whatever the weather, were always dressed in thick padded clothing that would have been necessary to face the bitter cold of a Russian winter, and perhaps they thought it was worth wearing in all weathers as it gave protection against the punishing blows they received.

One morning I witnessed a minor act of sabotage, and seeing that it was against the Germans, it was amusing to watch. At some distance outside the wire a new fence was being erected, probably to make the camp even more secure, and the task was being carried out by several Russians supervised by three armed guards. Unusually, the guards were taking a more practical part in the work, not the hard stuff, but indicating where the holes were to be dug and so on. This caused them not to be watching what all of the work party were doing at any one time, and, as each fresh hole was being dug, one of the Russians, who had managed to hang back unnoticed, was pulling up the posts that had previously been carefully set vertically in the holes, one at a time. With their attention firmly fixed on the one post being set, none of the guards looked up to take in the whole scene. The Rusky, as we called them, looked across occasionally and grinned broadly. Inevitably one of the guards would look up and around, and then the thick padded jacket worn by the culprit would be tested fully for its other qualities, but since it was time for our luxurious midday swede soup to be dished out, I did not wait for fear of missing it.

On another occasion as I and another prisoner were out enjoying the extra walking space around the camp in glorious sunshine, we heard a jingling noise. We immediately recognised the Camp Commandant in all his military splendour, driving a very smartly turned-out pony and carriage. We knew better than to ignore him, but what could we do? Somehow the correct procedure flashed into our minds, from those punishing weeks we had spent in the early days of training and square bashing. We simultaneously sprang to attention, did a smart left turn to face the rough track he was travelling on, and remained in that position while he passed by. The most we expected in recognition was perhaps a glance in our direction, and how he managed it without losing his balance, I don't know, but still holding the reins in one hand, he rose to his full height and gave, not the newly imposed Nazi salute, but a good and proper military one. We felt quite honoured.

Another incident has remained lodged in my mind. I can't remember which Stalag it was, but in the surrounding woods military exercises were constantly in progress. Occasionally we would catch sight of a Tiger tank and thought how frightening it must have been to face one in battle. One morning prisoners inside the toilet block, which was near to the wire, got a sample of their firepower, fortunately not the main gun, but from a machine gun. I was not there at the time, but I did get a dramatic account from someone who was. The toilet blocks were quite long, accommodating a number of people, but with no privacy of course. That was alright as one could sit and chat to a neighbour, but on this particular occasion tranquillity turned to panic when bullets came through the wall. Luckily, they must have travelled to almost the extent of their range before doing so, as they appeared to do no more than drop inside at the feet of the long row of people seated there. The whole place became empty very quickly. Some time later an official apology from the CO of the offending unit was posted up on the notice board; our Commandant must have taken some action on behalf of his prisoners, and to think we did not think he cared that much about us.

It must be said that the Commandants of each of the Stalags I was in appeared to be, in most ways, real professional soldiers and not Nazis. I think they had no control of the food rations, quantity or quality, but of course I did not have to deal with them, so I can only tell of some small and insignificant details that make me say that perhaps they were not too bad.

*

Our stay in Poland did not last long and we knew that we would more than likely be moved on again when we started to hear what must have been Russian guns in the distance.

We did not get too excited about liberation, however, having learnt our lesson in the previous camp and, sure enough, I believe it was around September 1944, there was a hasty but calmly executed evacuation and a march back to Torun railway station. Once there we found the goods trucks were waiting with the usual security measures in place, but this time we were packed in even tighter; there was barely room to stand.

Hardly able to see outside, it was a long time before we knew we were going in the obvious direction, westward. There was the usual waiting in sidings, even the guards did not know our final destination. This, the slow progress and the discomfort, must have made the journey seem much longer than it actually was, and as it got dark we moved into what appeared to be a huge marshalling yard. There was not enough room to lie down, so sleep was out of the question – even more so when anti-aircraft guns started firing and bombs could not only be heard but felt to be dropping not far away.

It was not long before the bombing intensified – we were in for a major raid. The doors were kept closed so no one could see if markers had been dropped or get any details whatsoever of what was going on. It was terrifying to sit there just waiting for a bomb to come through the truck roof or to be blasted away by a near miss. Being so cramped and securely detained added a fear of utter helplessness. No one spoke, we all knew what each other was expecting and just waited for it, and did not even think about food.

The bombing stopped, as it should have done in an RAF raid which went according to plan, almost as if it had been controlled by a switch. We, on the other hand, did not recover just like that and even if there had been enough room to lie down and sleep, it would have been impossible for some time. Thinking of the aircraft returning home after the raid, it occurred to me that Lancasters from my squadron could well have been among them, which reminded me yet again of my hopeless position; in the hands of the enemy, entirely at their mercy. Our boys, if they were lucky enough to get home safely, would have a good meal of bacon and egg waiting for them after de-briefing, and a good bed. Then the following evening, if they had been stood down from operations, they would be off to the pubs and cinemas of Grimsby followed by a fish and chip supper. It was painful to think about; but then the other possibility came into my mind: perhaps they would not get back safely and perhaps they would not be as lucky as I had been.

Early next morning we moved off again, and later that day arrived at our destination, Stalag 357, close to the small town of Follingbostel, thirty miles from Hanover, on the windswept plains of north-western Germany.

Stalag 357 was part of a large complex of camps based around the German barracks on the outskirts of Fallingbostel. I don't think it was newly built, but it could only have been partly occupied before our arrival. The combine I was with in Poland managed to get into a hut together, so we soon settled in. All the huts were very similar if not identical; the threatening Posten boxes were there, occupied by two guards, leaning on their machine guns ready to mow down anyone attempting to fight their way out through the wire, and the hopeless atmosphere that all prison camps have was certainly there. The swede soup would still only be eaten by starving men and we consumed it just as greedily. The one seventh of a loaf of black bread went no further to satisfy our needs, so things were much the same except our lifeline, the Red Cross food parcel supply, became more and more sparse. This was not because they were not despatched, but because of the damage being inflicted on the internal transport system by the Allied air forces, even the Commandant admitted this. A case of good news bringing bad news.

*

As the winter began to take over, the lack of the Red Cross parcels really began to show: people got even thinner and the ones who were normally just a little bit tubbier showed it most. Very few continued to walk the circuit, and no football games were played. Apart from roll call, when attendance was never excused, and perhaps a very quick wash, most of the day was spent lying in the bunks trying to keep warm.

The war news was good in France, with rapid progress being made, and on the Russian front, but in Belgium, in our direction, there always seemed to be holdups or even reversals. It seemed we would die of starvation long before liberation.

It began to seem that escape was our only chance of survival; dangerous thinking but it did seem that we were approaching a time when it would be a case of doing something or dying. A member of our combine had previously noticed that a small toilet block was unusually close to the wire and had often seriously discussed the chances of concealing oneself in the building until after dark, and then it would only be a short crawl to the wire, and as the soil was soft and sandy tunnelling under and out should not be difficult. This did not appeal to me at all, for one thing I had not forgotten two prisoners being shot dead attempting something similar at Stalag Luft VI. Also, no help would be forthcoming from the Escape Committee as it was already discouraged, if not totally forbidden by the powers that be, after D Day.

Despite this, the escape plan was given more thought, and we started to discuss the finer details. We would have to get some help from the Escape Committee and were about to approach them when a terrible thing happened. It was some time in the late evening when we heard two or three shots fired in the distance. No prisoners were allowed out after dark, so all we could do was hope that it was nothing serious, but it was.

Next morning at roll call it was announced that two prisoners had been shot dead while attempting to escape, but no further details were given. Later on, from other prisoners, we learned that it was at the exact spot where we were considering the possibilities of getting out. We were shocked to say the least but could not resist going to have a look where it had happened, and there we came across a terrible scene. There was blood and bits of flesh everywhere, which to some who claimed to know, proved that they were shot at very close range, not while running away, and they were certainly inside the wire. The whole incident was very sad and very shocking but when in the hands of such an enemy, there is no justice.

*

The winter of 1944-45 was the longest, coldest and by far the most miserable time of my life. Christmas Day brought no cheer, in fact it made things a lot worse by reminding everyone of what we were missing. We still got the BBC news but it gave no cheer, reporting the setbacks in the Ardennes area of Belgium, for what seemed an age. But then came news of that wonderful and courageous operation by the Paras, when they captured the bridge over the Rhine at Arnhem, and it raised morale beyond belief – it seemed that liberation was imminent. The main force, however, was not able to battle their way up to them, and the Paras had to surrender their gain after a fierce battle, so it was back to doom, gloom and helplessness.

A few days later we got some idea of what the Paras had been through in capturing the bridge. Having been taken POW, those considered fit enough to walk were brought into our camp; they all looked pitiful. They were all very dirty of course, but there did not seem to be one who was not wounded in some way, and on top of this, they had come at a time when we had nothing to give them, either in food or medical help. They were kept together in a distant part of the camp, so we did not have much contact with them. Dixie Deans, our Camp Leader, would have done all that he was able to in order to make them as comfortable as possible and none of us would have begrudged it if he could have found just a few Red Cross parcels from somewhere to help them in their plight.

*

As the better weather came, so too did news of the war improving. People got weaker and thinner, but a light was appearing on the horizon. Our forces, the British

Liberation Army, were actually on German soil and continuing to move towards us. We began to ask, 'How long will it be now?' The Germans have nowhere to move us to, we thought wrongly.

As always, the rumour circulated, followed by the reality that our hopes were shattered once again. Come early April 1945, we were on the move once more. No one had any idea where we were going, not even a rumour about that, but sure enough, section by section, hut by hut, the camp was being emptied. When it got to our row of huts, somehow I was able to make a decision that could have made the difference between life and death twice; first by stopping in the camp and later by going out with the others.

I don't know how I ever did it. I am not, and never have been, a brave person or a natural leader but standing outside with several others watching the prisoners being ousted out and then marched off, it occurred to me that this operation of moving us out was nowhere near as orderly as the previous ones. There was an atmosphere of haste and panic about it.

Once formed up outside in front of the hut, that group was quickly moved off somewhere and the same guards returned to empty the next hut, moving towards us. The doors of the emptied huts were left open, but none of the guards went back inside to check that they were now empty; it seemed that there was not time to do this. I stood there noting all this, with the same bitter disappointment that we were all suffering at not being liberated. It must have been this that led me into disregarding the dangers and only thinking of the benefits of the opportunity I thought I could see, and instantly wanted to put it into action.

With this optimistic attitude I quietly revealed its simplicity to four or five fellow POWs who were standing with me, and they were instantly convinced that it looked like a winner; so, we acted. We went back into the hut to try to make sure we had done all we could do, not in preparation to leave, but to stay.

The plan was so simple. When they came to empty our hut, which we knew they would in just a few minutes, we would make sure that we were at the tail end of the column that would be assembled outside. When it moved off, making sure that the two guards were in front of us and that we were opposite the door of, not the first empty hut, but to give the column time to get going, the third one, we would break away and slip quietly inside and immediately dive into the narrow gaps between the bunks, thereby concealing ourselves from anything but a thorough search.

This all went well and according to plan. All we could do for the first few minutes was to lie there, hardly daring to breathe, and hope that our action had not been spotted from the posten boxes. Gradually the whole area went quiet and we became a bit more comfortable. It was an unusual sort of escape, if that is what it turned out to be – don't leave the Stalag, let the Stalag leave you; but we certainly did not feel like cracking jokes as we were still very, very frightened. While we continued to lie between the bunks, not daring to get up, I started to think to myself, 'We are going to get away with this.' but then I remembered the dogs. I had not given them a thought in my plan, but now I thought, 'That is what they will do, send one or two guards round with dogs and they will soon sniff out anyone left behind.' I was back to being as terrified as I was when first starting to make the break.

A while passed and I began to get my confidence back as I had started to think that if they were going to check the hut they would have done so by now, as it was getting dark. Eventually I thought it safe to shut the door. Crawling across the floor, to make it less likely that I would be seen from the outside, I slowly and quietly did this. With the door closed we at least had a feeling of more security and, as long as we did it very quietly, we could talk together.

Without noticing, we had already gained something from our escapade – it had stopped us craving for food but the cravings soon returned, as they always did, and we decided to take stock. Fortunately, in the days before, when we had realised we would have to make a run for it at some point, we had manged to squirrel away what little spare food we could find. Luckily, a few Red Cross food parcels had got through fairly recently, allowing a quarter parcel per man, so we were comparatively well off for food as we made our bid for freedom. A little extra bread had also been issued because of the move; that meant there was no telling where or when the next issue would be.

Someone amongst us had remembered we would need some water – I had not thought about that either – and had found and filled a couple of Klim tins (dried milk from Canadian parcels).

When it was completely dark it was agreed that it was safe to get up from between the bunks and sit at a low level, facing each other, where we could talk quietly until it was accepted by all that it was now safe enough to have a very careful look outside. One brave person, not me, volunteered to do this. He was made for the job and hardly being noticed, even by us who were carefully watching, he disappeared. He returned shortly, just as stealthily, bringing the best possible news; there was nobody to be seen out there. There were no lights anywhere and, as far as he could see, the posten boxes were empty and there was no sign of activity at all. The escape plan until now could not have gone any better but we were assuming and relying on being liberated in a short while.

There were no longer any daily BBC news bulletins or even rumours – we could only conceal ourselves and wait, which we did for the next two and a half days. An occasional reconnaissance was carried out, but these only revealed what we thought we already knew – we were the only ones left in the whole camp. Actually, we were not. Years later I learned that the Germans had abandoned the intention of trying to move every prisoner from this vast camp and fled, leaving quite a number unguarded and uncared for in one far removed compound. This would have been out of our field of vision.

By this time, we were getting worried about our food supply. We were used to meagre rations but now there was nothing at all on the horizon, only the hope of a quick liberation. The truth, unfortunately, was emerging that we did not know when that would be.

*

Next came a dramatic change in the situation: some of the prisoners who had left our compound had been returned – not all of them came back – and their guards had gone off and left them unguarded. We later learnt that, with the advancing Russians and Allies, it was absolute chaos out there; not even the Germans knew where they were going, and some decided to return the prisoners to the camp before fleeing. This was wonderful news as it indicated that the Germans were losing control and we could emerge from hiding and mix with those returned. Any thought that our escape had achieved nothing, and that we might as well have gone out with the rest, was banished when we heard about their journey.

We were told of a horrific attack on the marching column by our own RAF Typhoons, firing rockets and then being strafed with cannon fire. Many who were in our hut had been killed or seriously wounded. It really stunned me to be told that one of those killed was a Canadian who I knew well. He was someone who could always raise your spirits when things were really bad, and to think he was one of those to be cut down, so cruelly, when freedom was so near, took some getting over. All who went on the march suffered badly. They were forced to keep going, but where to? Even the guards did not know. They had little food or water and had to try to sleep anywhere. Lucky ones were in leaky old barns that cattle were considered too precious to be kept in or a ditch, still wet from the winter rains. The more we mixed and talked to those who had been on the march, the more we appreciated how we had benefitted from going into hiding and staying put.

*

Our greatest fear now was not the return of the German forces, but that of starving to death. We were half starved before the move and now we were in a far worse position – there was nothing.

No Man's Land was often referred to in accounts of World War One by the veterans of that war, and it occurred to me that that was where we were now. Again, from hearing about that war, bitter fighting must be expected before our forces got to us, and how would we fare in that? Did our forces know exactly where we were? There did not appear to be any aerial reconnaissance in the day time or we would have been out there waving vigorously; it would have been some little thing to do to help ourselves. We had no idea of what to expect or what was expected of us.

At last something did happen; just after it got dark some five days after the part of the columns were returned, a terrific artillery barrage opened up: shells were passing directly overhead, and they sounded to be very low. The noise was unbelievable and to add to the terror, the hut, particularly the roof, was shaking so much it seemed that it would come crashing down on us, even if we did not receive a direct hit. The roof danger was somewhat self-inflicted as during the long cold winter the meagre fuel allocation to burn on the tiny stoves in the huts was stopped entirely; in desperation we allowed self-appointed structural engineers who, after some study of the structure while lying on a top bunk, decided which of the timbers could be removed with reasonable safety and burnt. The barrage continued with no let-up in its intensity until just before dawn. For the whole time, each second appeared to be our last, brought about by a near miss, a direct hit or from being trapped under the wreckage of the hut and left undiscovered.

I had experienced being bombed by the Luftwaffe in the earlier part of the London blitz, being shot down over Berlin, witnessed the terrible effect of carpet bombing by the USAAF in Frankfurt am Main, but I found that having artillery shells passing just overhead, for so many hours, was the most frightening experience by far. I fully understood what people who had suffered flying bomb and rocket attacks in London meant when they said of the two terrorising weapons, they would rather have the rockets, even if they were more devastating, because of the terrible nerve racking seconds between the engine of the flying bomb cutting out, and the explosion upon landing. They had seconds, which would have seemed like an age, to see who was going to get it.

Being young, we soon shook off the fear of the night's bombardment and getting some food became, once again, the most important thing. We were getting seriously hungry at this stage but where was there to look for food? The Germans had gone, any Red Cross parcel supplies were by now just a memory and there was no sign that we were about to be liberated. Everyone was very noticeably getting weaker. It took a great effort to get up from the bunk, and what was the point? None of the prisoners who had been out on the march would have anything to give away and it would have been very dangerous to venture out of the camp in search of food.

Later in the day the thought struck me that something edible might have been left in the German kitchen, a place prisoner would have had absolutely no access to normally, and this inspired me to get up and investigate. It turned out to be a wasted effort, there was not a scrap of anything inside, so I quickly returned outside, where I noticed a small heap of rotten small potatoes. With nothing at all to be found in the kitchen this miserable heap took on a new value, and getting down on my knees, I stirred up the rotting, slimy mass with my fingers, hoping that some still edible ones could be found. The smell was foul but that was no deterrent, and a few, considering the desperate need, were found that were at least part edible.

Back at the hut I was declared a hero when I returned with my dubious prize. The few rotting potatoes that I was able to find were eagerly washed and the bits that were really inedible chopped off. The wait for the remaining scraps to cook on the blower (a small homemade stove, with the fire boosted by a hand driven fan, based on the same principle as a forge, that had the essential quality of using only a minute quantity of fuel to boil water) was almost unbearable, but to a starving group like we were, it produced by no means a banquet, but a very welcome and much needed bit of nourishment.

*

In the past few days thousands of prisoners of all nationalities who had been on the march from other prison camps, were driven in desperation into Stalag 357. Fortunately, our compound, just a small part of this huge camp, did not become crowded. The few prisoners who were brought into our compound were mainly Russians who preferred to dig holes in the ground instead of going into near vacant huts. From somewhere they acquired rusted sheets of corrugated iron to cover them, making a kind of burrow, and, unbelievably, lit fire down inside them. They appeared perfectly content to live like this; presumably it was an improvement on what they had endured previously.

Soon after the potato feast, I became ill with a high fever and diarrhoea. I felt as though I was surely going to die; in fact, at one point I wished I could have done so. Throughout the night I had to get up to use the latrine. I blamed the potatoes, but early next morning one of our group, who had suffered no ill effects from eating the potatoes, came back to the hut with the bad news that there were many others suffering with similar symptoms in the compound.

He also had some good news – the British Medical Officer and some of his orderlies had returned to the camp, but there was a long queue waiting to see him. Ungratefully, I just groaned, but then thought this my only chance of survival. I laboriously donned every piece of clothing I had, wrapped a blanket around myself, and set off. Long before I got to the medical hut I was in a queue of many, all looking very ill. It was not just a case of waiting patiently, because every so often I was forced to leave the queue and find any sort of privacy to do what I had been doing all night. This was not such an impediment to progress up the queue because everyone had to do the same and, eventually, I reached the hard-working Medical Officer.

As expected, his surgery was very primitive. He sat at a bare table and in the background stood an orderly. The Medical Officer seemed to diagnose my complaint quickly; ruling out it being caused by eating the potatoes, he said I was suffering from dysentery and there was little he could do to help. With that, the orderly stepped forward offering two white tablets while the doctor said, 'Take these, go and lie down and keep as warm as possible.' Then it was 'Next please'. I struggled back to the hut thinking I had not gained much for my efforts and felt extremely deflated, but it was only the next day when the whole situation took a dramatic turn for the better.

Chapter 8

Liberation

I was lying prone on my bed when someone from the hut dashed in to say a British tank could be seen just outside the camp. The news immediately brought new life into me and I managed to get up and struggle outside to get a glimpse of this long awaited happening. I strained my tired eyes and there it was, moving very slowly towards us, appearing to be looking for something.

We knew, because we had spent many an hour gazing out beyond the wire at this farmland, that concealed in a barn which was integral with the farmhouse, was a Tiger tank. If only we could tell them, we thought, but this proved to be unnecessary. Machine gun fire was heard coming from the farmhouse and the British tank came to a halt. It could be imagined that they were thinking, 'Where did that come from?' Then the turret was swung slowly around and a shell was fired at the house, quickly followed by another. The farmhouse was reduced to a pile of rubble, but surprisingly there was no sign of the Tiger tank. It must have been moved at some time while we were locked in our huts, but the problem had solved itself and we had witnessed the first action towards our liberation.

The British tank did not continue to move towards the camp but veered off to go somewhere behind the ruins of the farmhouse. This was a little disappointing and nothing else happened that day. Exactly what we had expected was difficult to say. The only guidance anybody had would be based on what might have happened in World War One; hundreds of infantry men with bayonets fixed surging slowly forward, bitterly fighting for each yard. Our liberation did not appear to be happening at all like that, that's if it was happening at all.

As the excitement died away so too the temporary improvement in my health and, feeling dreadful again, I was glad to return to my bunk. Had I suffered an illusion? I thought, after only a short time. Was it something that happened with dysentery? Thankfully, I fell into a deep, undisturbed sleep, which lasted until quite a reasonable time the next morning, when I awoke feeling a bit better. One good thing about my illness was the craving for food was almost gone, and, although liberation was eagerly awaited, getting better was perhaps my priority.

It was around mid-morning, on April 16, 1945, as far as I can ascertain, when a great cheer rang out throughout the compound. At the time I was in the hut on my own, so I could not ask what it was all about.

Quickly though, two of the original escapees rushed in shouting, 'They are here. They are here.'

My health had improved further so I was able to react to this almost unbelievable news by getting up quite quickly, and, with a bit of urging from the boys, was able to hurry down to the main gate. Sure enough, there stood an armoured car, with its occupants unable to get out because of a cheering crowd surrounding it. When they eventually managed to disembark, our liberators were able to identify themselves as members of the Royal Irish Hussars, part of the 7th Armoured Division.

Soon after, other armoured vehicles of the same Regiment arrived, and there was a great deal of handshaking and backslapping. Gifts of food, cigarettes and chocolate bars were gratefully received, and the atmosphere of our prison was completely changed from misery and despair to one of hope and happiness within minutes. The way we were liberated was completely different to what I had visualised. Everything seemed so organised. The soldiers looked clean and, apart from their tin helmets and a varied assortment of arms at the ready, could well have been fresh from the barrack square. None were seen to be marching, there were vehicles of every description making up this highly mechanised spearhead.

Two soldiers of a Scottish regiment proudly pulled back the canvas cover of their 5cwt utility vehicle to show me inside. It was immaculate, with everything neatly stowed away and in pride of place, properly hung on hangers, were their full ceremonial dress uniforms.

There was not a lot of the sound of warfare that I was expecting to hear, except of course for the artillery barrage, only gunfire was in short bursts coming from many different directions, and not from a concentrated front all moving together, and that's how it continued for some days.

By the end of Liberation Day, I was feeling much better in health and the feeling of being free was really indescribable, but I could not instantly take food for granted. A soldier had given me a tin of corned beef that morning, we had also been assured by the Army that each man would be receiving the normal rations from tomorrow onwards, but even so, I carefully measured and ate one quarter of the meat, saving the rest just in case I awoke from a teasing dream.

*

The next morning we were asked, not ordered, to attend a meeting down by the main gates, where an Army officer introduced himself, saying it was his job to attend to our welfare. Then he started with a very serious warning about the uncertainty of the military situation around the camp. Explaining that while he could well understand that we would have a great urge to get out from behind the wire, he strongly advised that we be patient for a little longer because there was still strong enemy resistance close by. Only the road was known to be clear, but even that could come under fire at any moment.

This advice was followed for a few days. I think we were all quite content to gloat over the exciting rations that had already been delivered as promised, and just look out from the main gate at the terrific amount of military traffic that flowed past.

Once the sounds of warfare had moved further away, someone said it would be nice to have a fresh egg as well as the daily food ration. A farm could be seen across a valley about a quarter of a mile away, not the one the tank had attacked, so four or five of us thought it must now be quite safe to venture out to see what we could persuade the farmer to part with.

We found only women in the farmhouse and had to reassure them that we had only come to ask for eggs. We must have been a ragged looking lot but they produced around half a dozen eggs, and then we were off. As we were climbing the slope, back towards the camp, the noise of some movement was heard. We could only guess that it came from within a group of small trees just to our left, and then eight or nine German troops came out from the trees just below us. Our surprise was quickly outweighed by fear; we were like sitting ducks, completely unarmed and outnumbered. Whatever any of us had been taught, in our early days of training about fieldcraft, would have been forgotten, so it must have been just natural to drop to the ground and remain perfectly still, hoping that we had not been seen.

It seemed like ages, crouched there hardly daring to breathe, when another group emerged; this time British soldiers, armed with all sorts of automatic weapons covering the Germans in front of them. The Germans were prisoners who had just been taken. Momentarily, and rather stupidly, we thought we were in the clear, but how would our soldiers know we were not another group of the enemy? We certainly did not look like RAF personnel. Should we remain as we were, hoping that we would not be noticed? Wisely, one of us stood up with both hands in the air shouting, 'RAF prisoners of war.' The soldiers brought their prisoners to a halt and swung their weapons to cover him, then, carefully, we all stood up, holding our breath, waiting to see if we were going to be accepted or shot down.

Eventually they lowered their weapons, and only then did we slowly walk over to them. We felt very embarrassed at our stupidity, but any apologies were brushed aside and while two or three of the soldiers kept an eye on the prisoners, we were feted and showered with chocolate and cigarettes. Then, for me, came yet another fright. I had been talking to a corporal about being a POW, telling him about the hardest bits, when he suddenly pulled the sling of a Tommy gun he was armed with over his head and tossed the weapon over to me, saying what he thought about all Germans. Then, quite seriously, he said, 'Bump this lot off.' As I started to protest he went on to say, 'Go on, it's alright, nobody knows we have them.'

First there was the shock of how hot the gun was, then came the weight of it, but just the thought of killing these wretched young Germans with it, in cold blood, really made me feel sick. It was an unlawful execution, and I had no stomach for that. I knew instantly that I would sooner kill myself; I could not pass that gun back fast enough. Looking back, I like to think the corporal was joking, but I am still not sure. If I had done what we were all strongly advised, and stopped in the camp, the situation would not have arisen.

*

It had been agreed long before that if we were liberated, those who had been in captivity the longest should be the first to go back to Great Britain. As a comparatively new POW that put me well down the list. Now that liberation had come, we had been told apologetically that the process of getting us out of the war zone could be a lengthy one, as the roads were in a poor condition and advancing columns must have priority. This did not seem to be a great disappointment to anyone. We now had plenty of food, were released from the possibility of mass execution, the Army were doing more than we expected to make us comfortable, the weather was fine and, although all letters still had to be censored, we could write home.

The Major who was our guardian also censored our letters and he made sure there was as little delay as possible in getting them away. We could not have been in better hands. He cared for his own soldiers equally well. I saw this with my own eyes when I took my second letter to his makeshift office only to find him really upset. He was looking at an English newspaper; they were printed in Brussels and reached the front line only a day old.

'Just look at this rubbish,' he said, tossing the paper over to me, indicating the frontpage headlines. They proclaimed, in the largest of print, that the British Liberating Army were 'walking' through Germany, insinuating that there was no opposition. He went on, 'I've lost three of my best blokes this morning, just down the road. There is a bit of a wood down there and the SS are hanging on like maniacs. Right, they can stop there until the flamethrowers come up later, they will soon shift them. I am not risking any more of my men.'

I could tell that he was really upset at the loss of his soldiers and that he had taken the newspaper headlines as an insult to them; and I thought he was right.

I don't know if the press was encouraged to report with a bias towards optimism, but a typical report on a major RAF operation would tell of the damage inflicted on the target in detail, but the extent of our aircraft losses would be dealt with at the very end of the article, in as few words as possible. It may have been helpful to the morale of the nation, but many squadron commanders would have the very unenviable task the next morning of informing next of kin that their loved ones were missing, being as optimistic as possible, but knowing that the chances of them still being alive were slim; a detail never reported in the newspapers.

*

One afternoon, when we thought that all the surrounding territory was now safe, one of the regiment's military bands came into the camp and after setting up on the back of their lorry, proceeded to give us a wonderful half an hour or so of stirring music. Unfortunately, there came an enforced interval when machine gunfire broke out from somewhere close by; whether we were the intended target or not, no one waited to find out. It seemed that the band were used to this sort of thing as they dispersed in a much more orderly manner, to shelter under the lorry, than their audience who fled in all directions. In seconds it was all over, no casualties thank goodness, and in no time the band had reassembled, continuing on exactly from where they had left off, while we the audience took rather longer to regain our posture and start listening again.

As the next two or three days passed without further incident we were told that we could venture out in reasonable safety, so two or three of us walked to the local village or town of Fallingbostel. Once there we discovered a military warehouse packed with all sorts of items, mainly German army equipment, and, when I look back, if transport had been available, a fortune could have been made. There were all the kind of things soon to be sought after by collectors – Paratrooper boots, uniforms, helmets, badges, parachutes and arms as well as more everyday items such as spades, buckets, brooms and tableware, but all clearly marked with the German military insignia.

In the basement were large stocks of dried food, such as rice, barley, peas and sugar. With my obsession for food, or the fear of becoming short of it again, I had to take a quantity of each, even if the load was difficult to get back to the camp.

*

As the days went by, the feeling of being in captivity gradually wore off, but the great respect for food was still with me and remains to this day. Each daily ration was gratefully received, and any food not eaten was squirreled away beneath first my own bunk and then a nearby unoccupied one. When the great day of departure for the airfield finally came, I could not carry most of it, so it had to be left with the hope that some of the Russians would find it.

On another visit to Fallingbostel, a day or two later, I witnessed something that made me ashamed of our Russian allies. There was an old German civilian walking along on one side of the street and on the other side, there were two Russians. They crossed the road making towards the old man, gesturing, by one of them lifting the left sleeve of his tunic, that they wanted to know the time. The old German obligingly pulled out his watch to help, but as he did so one of the Russians grabbed the old man by the shoulders while the other snatched the watch and chain. They then walked off leisurely, smiling as they gloated over what they had stolen and, no doubt, looking for their next victim.

A second visit to the warehouse could not be resisted but, although only two days later, by then almost everything stored there had been made useless. The sacks had been slashed and their contents strewn about. The upper floors had been set on fire and the water used to quench the flames had drained down to ruin all the dried food in the basement. I could not add to my already more than adequate store back at the camp, which was just as well, for the next morning I discovered my name was on the list to join the next party to be returned to Great Britain.

Although liberation had brought about a wonderful change in our lives, the majority of us were civilians at heart, and that was what we wanted to return to being. It was the simple things of that life such as going to the pictures (the cinema), playing darts at the local pub, watching the local football team playing in the park on a Saturday afternoon and having a slap-up breakfast on a Sunday morning when you did not have to race off to work, these were the things we had craved to be reunited with. And, of course, there was Adelaide.

*

At last we were told to make our way into Fallingbostel, from where we were taken to an airfield not too far away to begin the process of repatriation. The transportation was well organised and for once it was nice to be treated like human beings and not cattle. There was no luxury, of course, we travelled in the back of lorries that stood very high above the ground, but to be helped to get up into them, instead of being prodded into them with rifles and bayonets, felt so much better. Being so high up caused a bit of a fright when it came to crossing a river, which was very wide and in flood. It must have been the Elbe and the original bridge across it, which had been destroyed, had been replaced by a pontoon one. This appeared, as we approached, very stable and safe, but as our lorry drove onto the first pontoon it heeled over to an alarming angle under the weight, and, because we were so high up, it seemed that we were going to be thrown straight into the river. As the crossing continued I think we all gained a bit of confidence in the safety of the bridge but were glad when we reached the opposite bank.

As the journey continued there was much more evidence of the bitter battles that had taken place, with burnt-out tanks and all sorts of other military vehicles. We saw buildings completely destroyed, and yet there were some villages showing no obvious signs of damage at all, but there were no signs of life in the streets.

Our destination was a huge airfield at a place called Diepholz, which certainly showed the scars of war. There were hundreds of what would have been either shell or bomb craters that had now been filled in to put the airfield back into service for use by the Allies. On one edge of the airfield tents had been erected and after a good meal this was where we spent the rest of the day and slept the night. There was no activity to watch from where we were, or even the noise of taking-off and landings, but the next day was different. I did not sleep well in the tent, it was quiet enough and lying on the ground was quite comfortable and warm, so it must have been the excitement of being on the way home that caused me to get little sleep that night.

When morning broke I was ready to get up and out of the tent quite early. The weather had remained fine and quite warm for several days and the morning gave the promise that it would continue to be very pleasant. Breakfast was served from a tented kitchen and eaten standing up. This, of course, was no hardship, in fact a luxury, it had been a long time since I was handed any sort of a meal, especially on a plate.

From far across the airfield aircraft engines could be heard starting up and then the aircraft could be seen moving. They were Douglas Dakotas, designed as a civil airliner, but adapted very successfully in many forms to be the workhorse of all the Allied air forces. After the war, like millions of human beings, it resumed its peace-time role and served excellently for many years before it could be bettered.

Soon the Dakotas were taking off and heading westwards towards Great Britain at quite frequent intervals, but as the day wore on it seemed that our party would not be going that day and we became resigned to the fact. However, we were then informed that because the weather was remaining good, the crew of one of the Dakotas had volunteered to do another trip that day. The weather of course had to be right, but it was the crew who really made it possible and they had to be backed up by the groundcrews at each end of the journey. I am afraid that when young, such things are taken for granted; we should have expressed our gratitude at the time for their contribution towards getting us home safely and a day earlier.

Once onboard the aircraft, it could be seen that this particular Dakota was fitted out for dropping

Paratroopers. On each side, inside the fuselage, were seats running the entire length with just a gap on each side for loading and, what must have been very much on the mind of the Paras when going on an operation, also for exit. I thought about it several times on that flight, trying to imagine what their feelings would have been. There would have been no ifs or buts; they would not be coming back with that aircraft. At a certain point they would be ordered to attach a line from their parachute pack to a static line above that ran the entire length of the fuselage. The doors would then be opened and, from a standing position, the Paras would follow each other to jump out. This was the point I thought about most; they were not jumping to save their lives, they could well be jumping to get killed.

As I mentioned previously, before the war only a tiny percentage of ordinary people had flown in an aircraft and most of my fellow passengers had been captured early in the war while fighting in the desert, not having had a chance to fly; so, on this first flight they must have suffered some apprehension, and this showed when a crew member, who I thought was the pilot, left the cockpit and walked down offering everyone sweets and chocolate. With distinct terror in his voice, my neighbour shouted to me, 'Who was that? Was he the pilot?' I felt quite knowledgeable when I was able to reassure him that there would be a second pilot, or possibly we were on automatic for a while.

Chapter 9

The White Cliffs of Dover

Another very thoughtful gesture was made by the pilot, if indeed it was he who had handed out the sweets, that was to send our spirits soaring. Unknown to us passengers at that stage, we were heading for an RAF station in Buckinghamshire, so he must have deliberately diverted a touch to the south and, making sure we were all looking forward through the cockpit by getting another crew member to draw our attention, he flew straight towards and then over the White Cliffs of Dover. It was a heart-wrenching sight, and I could almost hear Dame Vera Lynn singing her famous wartime song. I did not, however, notice any bluebirds flying over them.

We landed, late evening, at RAF Wing, and members of the WAAF met us and escorted us to a reception area that was set up in the open; even the weather was continuing to be kind to us. I did not kiss the ground as I always thought I would, but I do remember being very aware of my footsteps when first leaving the aircraft and thinking, 'This is what I have been waiting for.'

At the reception area medical orderlies dusted us with a white powder. No area was left untreated and one by one we were turned into something like snowmen. I suppose we would have been a rough looking bunch and needed to be treated with caution. Everybody was so kind and patient, especially as our arrival had not been expected. Next came the novelty of being seated at a real table on real chairs for some refreshments, which we saw off in no time at all. We then queued to see a doctor, which of course was a necessity, but this process revealed the only lack of thought or organisation that I ever noticed during the whole process of being received back home, and even that made for a bit of comedy. A temporary medical centre had been set up with about six cubicles curtained off to give privacy and in each one there was a medical officer in attendance. I was making my way into one of them, after being called, when the canvas door of one further along burst open as the patient made a very hasty exit. Following close behind came the medical officer, a woman, shouting, 'Don't be so damned ridiculous.' I have to explain that in 1945 lady doctors were quite rare and for a man, who might well have rarely seen a woman for possibly four or five years, and then only in the far distance, to be expected to submit himself to being intimately examined by one, was perhaps a little unthoughtful. I don't know how the problem was resolved because after my examination, by a man, all was quiet and orderly again and we were reassembled to await transport to the nearest railway station.

I think at this stage Army and RAF personnel must have been separated because the train I boarded went straight to RAF Cosford; Army personnel must have gone to another establishment. I hope they were treated as well as we were. RAF Cosford was the RAF's main medical centre in those days, so I suppose they were somewhat used to handling people in need of help, and although it was by now around two in the morning, we were certainly well received.

We were shown to our accommodation, which had been obviously well prepared, set down anything we might have been carrying and then a bathroom was ready, with the water already in the bath at the right temperature, for each one of us. Large white towels were there waiting for after we had indulged ourselves in a luxury some had not experienced for four or five years. It was a lovely feeling to be submerged in the warm water and leisurely cleanse oneself. Returning to the room where we were to sleep, the top covers of the beds had been turned back, pyjamas were there waiting, and within minutes I was enjoying a sleep that I was to remember for the rest of my life.

It would be eleven o'clock before I awoke next morning, and before I could convince myself that all this luxury was not a continuation of a dream, I was rewarded with what might be described as revenge – on the very RAF Flight Sergeant who had made our lives hell when I was attending my first Signals School. You may remember me telling you that we all lived in fear of him, yet the extraordinary thing, right there, was that this very Flight Sergeant was now offering me, humble me, still lying in a nice warm bed, a mug of delicious hot steaming tea. The coincidence was unbelievable, and I could not help telling him where we had met before. He declared in quite a friendly tone of voice that he thought he could remember me before mentioning the time and place – extraordinary.

The day went on to be quite a busy one. Everyone was fitted out with complete new uniforms. Further, more detailed medical inspections were made, some interrogation into how our aircraft was shot down, and as to how I was treated as a prisoner of war. I also had the opportunity to suggest any improvements to the means of escape from the Lancaster. I did this vigorously because the sight of three of my crew trapped there, not able to get out, was still very much in my mind, and always will be.

Later in the day we were given money; notes and loose change. The coins seemed to be so heavy in the pocket, it took days to get used to carrying them again. What could we buy with them? This presented another problem but, as it became evening, that one was solved. Cosford was a large RAF station, built between the wars, and had its own cinema, so most of us followed the crowd to partake of a pleasure that had not been available for so long.

Back in those lovely beds, with plenty of space around them and the clean white sheets, the second night soon passed, and now it was Sunday. There were still a few more formalities to be got through, badges and ranks to be attached to the new uniforms, and travel warrants issued. We even had our individual train times sorted out for us – we were treated like kings.

When we thought that they could not do any more to help us, one member of staff even remembered that we would not have any handkerchiefs. These were never an RAF issue, but some were found and given out; and that was not the end of the care and attention. During our short stay at Cosford the weather had changed completely. It got very cold and just before we were due to leave, it started to snow. Now, according to RAF rules and regulations, Summer started on May 1st and today was the 2nd but, in defiance, greatcoats were produced and issued. We were spoilt beyond belief.

*

By mid-day the whole group was very self-consciously standing on the platform awaiting the train to Wolverhampton and from there to our various home towns. It was a strange feeling: I was delighted to be on the last lap towards what I had been craving for all this time, but I felt very much on my own now and facing a world that seemed to have changed while I was away. I was glad of the greatcoat, not only because of the inclement weather, but it had extra comfort about it; it was something that had not changed. I could wrap myself up in it until I had got the hang of things again and got a bit more confidence back.

My parents had moved out of London since I joined the RAF, which was a good thing because of the bombing and the terrible flying bomb and rocket attacks that followed, but rural Huntingdonshire, where they now lived, was not so handy, or anywhere near so exciting as my old familiar haunts that I so much wanted to get back to. Fortunately, my married sister, who lived quite close to the old home, could always be relied upon to put me up (I have long ago realised what an imposition this was, to put me up for a night or two when on leave), so I decided to make her my first port of call; unbeknown to me that decision formed part of a remarkable coincidence.

By the time I had made my connection at Wolverhampton and arrived at Euston it was dark. That was a good thing because I did not feel quite so conspicuous. The streets were now lit again, the chances of more air raids by conventional aircraft I suppose had been ruled out, but hardly to the pre-war standard, so I could still hide a bit in the gloom, and that, strangely, is what I felt I wanted to do.

I had no trouble in remembering my way about and that there was a local LMS electric service, Euston to Watford, that would take me to where my sister lived. I was beginning to 'get back in', but the streets were so much quieter than I thought I could remember them, with hardly any people walking about. I did pass a woman I knew slightly, and it was a little reassuring when she showed some recognition.

Arriving at my sister's house there was some delay after ringing the doorbell. In those moments my confidence waned again. Had my sister moved during my absence, or something worse? I did notice a lot more bomb damage had taken place, but all was well, in fact more than well, because my home coming, entirely by coincidence, had coincided with a family gathering and beyond my wildest dreams – Adelaide was there too.

She had got in touch with my family after her letters to me were returned to her by the Squadron and was later told by my sister that I was a prisoner of war. That information was first picked up by my brother who, when I was reported missing, started listening to a radio programme transmitted from Germany presented by a person who called himself Lord Haw Haw. He cunningly included, at intervals during his programme, the names of newly taken prisoners of war, knowing that this would attract an audience of anxious next of kin hoping to gain news of loved ones reported missing. Ninety-five percent of the broadcast would be taken up by exaggerated claims of German successes in battle, aimed at demoralising the British listeners. Lord Haw Haw was a British traitor, his real name was William Joyce. He was brought back to England to face trial at the end of the war in Europe and was hanged at the Tower of London.

My arrival, coinciding with the family gathering and, best of all, Adelaide being there too, was truly remarkable. It could not have been better if it had been carefully planned. My mother had received my letters sent after I had been liberated and passed the news around the family, but nobody could say in advance when I would arrive home. Adelaide was on her way back to Gloucestershire, after spending most of a ten day leave at her home, and had called to see my sister on the way, not even knowing that I had been liberated.

I rang the doorbell and waited. It was opened by my sister and on seeing me they shouted, 'He's home. He's home.' Then Adelaide walked forwards to see what the commotion was, and our eyes met. Though we had left each other madly in love, we just didn't know what to say.

I would like to report that my first words, spoken to my fiancée after so long apart, were of the romantic variety, but I glanced at the new stripes on the sleeve of her WAAF uniform and said, 'Flight Mech,' followed by 'Eh?' She had been promoted to the position of flight mechanic.

Later, while the ladies of my family, despite the even more severe rationing that people were now having to endure, were busy preparing a welcome home meal, Adelaide and I were able to get reacquainted and within minutes it seemed that we had never been parted.

Adelaide's leave was due to expire in two days, so in the circumstances and after much deliberation, she sent a telegram, that was the usual way to communicate quickly in those days, asking if her leave could be extended by forty-eight hours. Within a day the reply was back – seven days compassionate leave granted, plus forty-eight hours. That was far more generous than expected and we were more than grateful for that concession.

During those ten lovely, carefree days together there was no question of 'Shall we go ahead and get married?', it was just a matter of 'When?'. September sounded promising but, of course, before then we both had to return to duty.

The RAF, to a great extent, had now lost its purpose. Germany surrendered unconditionally a few days after my return. The war in the Far East continued with unceasing vengeance, but it seemed that it was not necessary for the bomber and fighter squadrons based in Britain to be transferred there, so our aircraft were now being reduced to scrap metal. In many cases that was being done by the very ground and air crews who only a few weeks before had been proudly flying and maintaining them. Most of these beautiful aircraft were smashed to pieces in a most undignified way with crowbars and sledgehammers; it was not a pretty sight to watch.

*

I was later told to return to RAF Cosford and once at the base, almost the first person I saw was David. He looked just as I remembered him on the squadron and, as usual, he was smiling and looking pleased with life, but he had suffered as I was soon to learn when he told me about the journey from Stalag Luft VI to Gross Tychow. A little later he was able to show me the bayonet wounds to his back and, although they were inflicted a year before, they were still very nasty to look at. He went on to tell of the much harder life prisoners were subjected to, compared with Stalag Luft VI, and then the appalling sufferings he endured while being marched aimlessly during the last weeks before liberation in atrocious weather conditions, with little or no food and water. I was spared all this, simply by being on the opposite side of K Lager at Stalag Luft VI, and then by dodging from one hut to another while being moved out of Stalag 357 at Fallingbostel – I never realised the dividends that would pay.

I was also, upon returning to Cosford, reunited with now ex-prisoners who I had been with at both Stalag

357 and Stalag Luft VI, but it took some time to realise who they were. Not only did they appear much wider and thicker, but also much taller. They were all smiling and radiating confidence. Their recovery was remarkable.

Back at Stalag Luft VI there was some organised entertainment in a building the Germans had allowed prisoners to adapt as a theatre. All tastes were catered for, but on the lighter side an ex-professional comedian was always popular, and his name was Ross Jones. During those few days when we returned to Cosford, enjoying a fine summer visiting Wolverhampton with David, we bumped into Ross Jones. We reminded him of how we knew him and were told that while he also was back at Cosford, with official permission, he had already got himself a week's work at the local Empire Theatre. Thereupon, he reached into his pocket and produced two complementary tickets for the show, about to start!

A few days later, which were spent with more medical checks and form filling, we were sent back on leave indefinitely and told to await further orders, and I headed home.

*

I was able to spend two days with Adelaide where she was stationed, having kindly been granted permission by her CO to be there. While there I received a telegram telling me to report to RAF West Milling in Kent but with no further details. I knew West Malling to be a fighter station, or so it was in the war, and wondered why I was going there. On arrival David was already there and I learned from him that we were to have a course of rehabilitation. I imagined all sorts of strenuous exercising and even revision in square-bashing but was soon to learn it was going to be just the opposite.

As the course assembled, several familiar faces appeared. Most of them also thought they were here to be knocked back into shape until we met the CO and his staff, who all had a most friendly and helpful manner. It turned out that we were to have a most interesting and enjoyable two weeks, with most of the time spent visiting the workplaces of local industry, but also benefitting from some wise and helpful counselling. The visits were to a sweet factory with generous samples provided, a brewery only previously dreamed about by most, the Short aircraft factory at Rochester, where the famous Sunderland was still in production, and Croydon aerodrome.

Croydon was one of the few airports in the country and it served London before Heathrow was ever thought of. What made it so interesting was the national airline of that time – British Overseas Airways Corporation, was struggling to create and maintain air services across the world. There were no civilian airliners being manufactured, so RAF planes were being modified to pioneer the new routes that were being allocated, until more suitable aircraft became available. Profitability could not be considered at this stage. It was explained to us that the Dakota was by far the most suitable because it was designed as a civilian aircraft, however it only had a short range. So, with great interest, we watched Lancasters being modified to fly the long-distance routes. Economic efficiency could not be considered. If the opportunity was not taken up immediately, to establish a route, it could be lost for ever. Consequently, the Lancaster, in its modified form and renamed the Lancastrian, would fly the Australia route in several hops. It would need a crew of four to transport only five passengers. We never guessed what a great industry was going to be developed from these makeshift aircraft.

The Dakotas were already flying regular services to some continental capitals, including Brussels, and this was seen as a great opportunity by two of our party. They had been shot down over Belgium in a Halifax and had been sheltered by the Resistance with a family there. Cheekily they asked if there was a chance of a free flight. This was granted with the approval of our CO who was with us on the visit.

*

Back at West Malling, David and I made plans to visit the families of the crew who had not survived. Although we knew we should do this, and wanted to, we were quite apprehensive about it, so sought some advice from the CO. He encouraged us to go ahead, but wisely pointed out that we could not assume that our crew were all dead, so warned we must be careful.

The visits were not nearly so difficult as we thought they would be because the families were so brave. They had accepted that the worst had happened and did not ask for details of how their sons or husbands had died. Each family made us very welcome, which made us feel much more comfortable with our task.

David was also able to make contact with Bob Brown, our Canadian crew member, confirming that he had survived – he had recovered from leg wounds and was now back home and looking very well in a photograph he sent.

*

Eventually, after some more leave, and with aircrews no longer being in demand, I was posted to Cranwell, the original home of RAF Signals, to serve out the final period of my war service – it was to be more than a year before I was a civilian again and able to return to coachbuilding – helping to train members of the Royal Dutch Navy to become air operators.

During my time at Cranwell weekend leave could be taken for granted, so Adelaide and I were able to see each other regularly and, with the war in the Far East coming to an end, making our future far more predictable.

Chapter 10

Wedding Day

September 29, 1945, started out looking like anything but a promising day weather-wise; it was quite cold for early autumn. There was a thick fog slowing down the London traffic as my Best Man, also my best friend, and I made our way to St Pancras railway station to catch the train to Market Harborough. It was my wedding day.

Fortunately, because of the timing of the buses we had no option other than leave in good time to catch the train. Hailing a taxi to take us to the station was not even considered in those days, that was still only something the rich did, even on such an important journey. Not long after the start of the rail journey we knew we were going to be late in reaching our destination, the train was barely maintaining thirty miles an hour because of the fog, but, with the unfounded optimism of youth, we did not panic.

At Adelaide's house her mother, on seeing the fog, had already expressed her doubts that Ron and I would arrive on time. However, later on in the morning, the fog rapidly disappeared. Our train was able to safely make up some of the lost time and we arrived in the village with enough spare time to have a quick drink in the Red Lion, before taking up our places, as rehearsed previously, inside the Parish Church in Sibbertoft.

As the pews filled up behind me I began to feel quite nervous and was glad when the organ struck up and I could get up and look back down the aisle and see Adelaide, looking absolutely lovely, on the arm of her father, coming slowly towards me. As we joined up, completely forgetting the onlookers, I gave her a saucy wink and a smile. Then all was well.

The reception was held in the close-by village school where Adelaide had attended as a pupil until the age of eleven. An excellent wedding breakfast was made possible by the generosity of friends and relatives who for some weeks had managed to save small amounts from their meagre weekly food ration; it was in all ways a truly village wedding.

*

After a honeymoon in Wales it was, for both of us, a return to RAF life and duty, but we could continue to see each other at weekends, and then with the help of a colleague, who was long established at Cranwell and very well connected there, we were introduced to a family in a nearby village who had a two-room accommodation to let. It was a rare opportunity indeed.

According to the rules of release from wartime service after the war came to an end, Adelaide, now a married woman, could claim immediate release, so in a short time we moved in.

Now the war was over in Europe and the Far East, life in the RAF was quite different. The terrific pressures that had been imposed upon all the military leaders to bring victory were now over, but our civil leaders had to face the problem of getting the millions of people who had either been conscripted into service or had volunteered to join the armed forces, back to what they had been fighting for – a normal peaceful civilian life. For many reasons this had to be a slow and carefully controlled process, known as demobilisation, and everyone other than the regulars were given a demobilisation group number. Age and length of service was considered to determine this. The lower the number the sooner release was granted. I was twenty-three and had joined up in September 1941, so I was allocated group 44. The slow pace of demobilisation caused discontent for those wanting to get back to civilian life, and this must have created a bad atmosphere for the regulars, who formed only a slim minority, wanting to get on with their chosen career.

I was content to stay at Cranwell for the time being. The living accommodation that we were lucky enough to acquire proved to be very satisfactory. Adelaide got on very well with our landlady and found plenty to do while I was on duty. Weekends were always duty free, so we could visit her parents if we wished or could visit Lincoln, Newark or Sleaford. Not on a spending spree as there was nothing to buy.

There did come a temptation to give up this comfortable life when it appeared on Daily Routine Orders that experienced aircrew were required as volunteers to take part in what came to be known as the Berlin Airlift. Some of the now redundant heavy bombers were having to be used to take vital supplies to the British Sector of Berlin, all land access being denied by the Russians. There was a good bounty payable, but it also entailed a three-year engagement. This and the appreciation of how comfortable my life was at Cranwell – I certainly would not be able to come home to my wife every evening – easily outweighed my desire to get back to flying duties.

The full wisdom of my decision was not revealed until years later, when the number of aircrew who lost their lives while carrying out that long operation was revealed; it was considerable but seemed to get little official recognition. It appeared I had, once again, made the right decision.

Epilogue

Reflection

I was demobbed in December 1946. My RAF training had taken over two-and-a-half years, had involved hundreds of hours of tuition and Britain's resources, but had ended abruptly, on only my third flight in anger. But I had completed the task for which I had been trained.

As air crews we were all too aware of the time ratio between training and operational flights. We used to say, 'The Air Ministry say that all the training given to air crew was worth it – even if you only managed to drop just one load of bombs on Germany.'

They never mentioned about getting us back home afterwards though.

As for my time behind the wire, I suppose you can benefit from anything life throws at you; the experience. The comradeships were a big positive from my time in the POW camps; when it was all over, of course, while there, you hated every day of it. But when you come back, you think of the people you knew there, what characters they were.

It's always been on my mind, how lucky I was to have been blown clear of that aeroplane when I was just twenty-one years old and all set to die. I often used to wake up in the night thinking about it all but I'm a very positive person; others didn't fare so well afterwards. But a lot of them went through far worse than I did.

As well as my demob suit, I came out of the war with some recognition for risking life and limb as my time in Bomber Command earned me the 1939-45 Star. I also became a life member of the Caterpillar Club, which has only one criterion for membership – that you must have saved your life by the use of a parachute.

My crew are always on my mind. I especially think of them on the eleventh hour of the eleventh day of the eleventh month, but I also think of them all the time. I have remembered them all my life and I will never forget them.

I once went to St Clement Danes Church in London, which is a memorial church to all those who have lost their lives serving in the RAF, and there's a great big book of remembrance there; each day they open it to a different page. Quite by coincidence, when I visited it was open on a page containing the names of some of my crew. It really got to me; it made me really cry.

For the record the names of my fallen friends found in that book are:

James Tosh (Pilot)
Jock (Hugh) Mosen (Navigator)
Reg Morris (Bomb Aimer)
Dick Walton (Rear Turret Gunner)

They are all laid to rest in the Berlin
1939-45 War Cemetery.

This book is dedicated to their memory.

Real Stories

Old Soldiers Never Die
FRANK RICHARDS

Old Soldier Sahib
FRANK RICHARDS

GEORGE BRINLEY EVANS
where the flying fishes play

THE SONGBIRD IS SINGING
SCENES FROM A WELSH CHILDHOOD IN THE 1920S
BY ALUN TREVOR

PARTHIAN

www.parthianbooks.com